Getting BACK UP

A Message of Hope

RAYE

Quantum Discovery
A LITERARY AGENCY

Getting Back Up
Copyright © 2023 by Raye

ISBN
978-1-960197-46-7 (Paperback)
978-1-960197-47-4 (eBook)
978-1-960197-45-0 (Hardcover)

Getting Back Up

A Message of Hope

Table of Contents

Introduction

One of the first things that God has ever said to me clearly was, "My sheep know my voice." I heard him calling to me one day and he said to me that if I opened up my mouth that he would speak. "I will expose you; I will strip you down for the world to see. They will see you in your nakedness, but they will see me in my Glory. I did not clean you up for you; I cleaned you up so I could use you." To God be the Glory! I pray that the Holy Spirit has His way with this pen and me. I pray that if only one person reads this book, that it is one soul that turns to God for the answer. He and only He is able to save a mess like me. Maybe you have not been through the same way, but if you're living, you're going through. If you read this book and don't find yourself in it somewhere read it again. I trust you will not only find yourself, but you'll find God carrying you. As you go on this journey with me allow yourself to identify with the pain and focus the delivering power of Jesus Christ, our Lord.

Just 'When Everyone Thought I was Dead

There were no vitals
All signs of life were gone
I was going to leave this life
To travel to the world beyond

There was no hope
For I saw the flat line
I was willing to walk away
Leaving this life behind

Leaving my children motherless
Breaking my mother's heart
Ready to go because I felt
That I had done my part

Just when everyone thought I was dead
Even I had given up on me
They were making plans for the kids
And paying my Insurance Policy

Just when everyone
Thought I was dead
The pallbearers were already named
Anger, Resentment, Fear
Rage, Guilt and Shame

They were ready to carry me
And take me to the earth
But Jesus intervened
And started my rebirth

Just when everyone thought I was dead
My Father stepped in and said, "Not so,"
Breathed his spirit into my body
Gave me bread so I could grow

God gave me a Savior
I call him Jesus Christ
Though the wages of sin was spiritual death
The gift of Salvation is Eternal Life

Eulogy of a Sinner

Here lies Tammy Burke, 04/23/66-7/24/95

Mother of two, wife of too many, Drug Addict, Adulterer, Murderer, Liar, Fornicator, Homosexual, Thief, Prostitute, and Child Abuser

She was married December 29, 1984. When things did not work out, Tammy had gotten hooked on drugs. As a drug addict Tammy would lie, steal and prostitute for drugs. While using, she was too trifling to use birth control so when the inevitable happened she killed her unborn babies because it wasn't convenient, Murderer. The children that did manage to survive were born out of wedlock, which not only made Tammy a fornicator, but also an adulterer. The children that survived, she poisoned their unborn bodies with crack. That was child abuse.

When someone dies it is left up to the world to speak your works over your body. Most of the time they will only tell the good things. What if your life was like my life and most of it was a nightmare? People wouldn't dare speak of these things at a funeral. All of a sudden everything was all right and they are going to heaven,"This is a Home Going Service," they would say.

When I attend funerals I always wondered why preachers always say that the departed, departed dearly and that they are going home. If they shut their eyes and they have not accepted the gift of salvation, which was given freely to us by God and only through our Lord and Savior Jesus Christ, then they are going home all right. I just can't imagine where this home may be, certainly not in Heaven. I don't mean to condemn anyone. I have not a Heaven or Hell to place anyone in. My story is for the hopeless. When all is lost and you are at the end of your physical strength, that's where God usually takes over and only if you let him. God can and will forgive everyone who seeks Him and who is willing to turn from wickedness. No matter who you are; no matter what you've done; When Jesus finds you and you make Him your Lord and Savior, your life is far from over.

If preachers tell the truth at funerals, more people would get saved. For this is the way that death serves life. What could you learn from this person's life? Bad or good there is a lesson in life and it's not just for you. I pray that when I die, someone has the boldness to tell the truth about me, and that is all of the above. But, nobody could ever tell this story about Tammy's death without telling the rest.

One day when Jesus was walking by, He found this dirty rag lying in the gutter. I mean life had crushed this rag so far to the earth until it was lower than anything you could imagine. He took this filthy rag that seemed to have no earthly use at all and said, "I will use this rag to glorify my Father." Everybody that walked by and saw this rag in the street will be a witness to my Father's great power. He held this rag in His hand all the way home like He had found something precious.

Everyone had walked pass and saw me in the gutter. My family had given up on me, and I had even given up on myself. One day Jesus picked me up, and breathed life into my corpse. The best description given was by my grandfather. He said that I looked like death eating an onion pickle. I was rotten to the core and that meant that a total recreation had to take place. God was going to make me a new creature.

But first, the surgery! Before anything is recreated, it is first tom apart, stripped down to the root. And if the root is bad, it has to be completely replaced.

Chapter One

BIRTH OF THE NEW CREATURE

Now, according to my own understanding, I just got tired of living the way that I was and I just did something about it. I didn't even recognize that this was a job that no one could do, but God, despite the six treatment centers that I had attended prior. To this program, I gave all of the credit. That was o.k. I guess. When I started out I tried to work the twelve-step program, but I didn't include God in this process. It was a matter of time before I would fall again. Ten months to be exact. The program suggested that I get a sponsor. Your sponsor could be anyone but yourself. I had a wonderful sponsor, but the damage was so deep. I couldn't get totally honest with her about what was in my heart because no one but the creator knew how damaged I was.

Suppose you had a pretty car. You treasured this car. But, one day it got stuck on the tracks and a train came by and totaled your pretty car. A Mercedes Benz and you could not afford another one. So you wanted to have it fixed. This car couldn't be recreated by none other than the manufacturer that originally designed the car.

1

I had to go back from whence I came. I've also heard it said in the fellowship that I attended that I only have to change everything. One day God must have said, "We only have to change everything" and He meant everything. I thought that all I wanted was to stop smoking crack. This was my only goal. I had no idea that God had His hands on me and that He never does anything partially. He is a God of wholeness and completion. So whoever is waiting for me to come out of the Repair Shop will be waiting for a very long time. The question must have been asked by God "Is there any insurance?" That's when my Jesus must have said, "Yes, I've paid it all."

About three years into my recovery I thought that I was all right. I thought so much of myself and the fact that I had come all that way. While giving some credit to others, I still felt a strange since of self-fulfillment. Everyday that I so called lived without a drink or drug was great, but there was something that just wouldn't let me be complete and I had gotten real comfortable with this thing. God created in me a hunger for something more. God said, "I mean everything"! I looked like I was clean. My appearance could fool anyone, even me. But I could not fool God. I claimed to have known Him all of my life. I didn't know Him, but thank God, He knew me inside out and The Master told me, "I'm not finished with you yet."

I remember when I met Jesus. I remember seeing Tammy the way God saw me and that scared me to life. When God showed me myself I wanted to run away as fast as I could and not look back. "Jesus, I don't want to ever see her again!" He told me, "One Last Look, Tammy.

If you don't look back, how will you see where I brought you from? If you don't see the salvation of the Lord, you won't give me the Glory." "But come on here, Jesus, I am anxious to live my new life." Jesus asked me, "What life are you talking about; your life? NO! You laid your life down. You did everything you could to kill yourself. Your life does not belong to you anymore, it belongs to God."

Chapter Two

ONE LAST LOOK

As I write these pages, know that I am dying to self with every stroke of this keyboard. The Holy Spirit is allowing me to share some things with you in truth that I would rather just forget about. I have found my purpose for being on the earth and that is to glorify my Father, which is in heaven. The key to living again was dying. The key to freedom from active addiction was honesty. The key to my soul's salvation was the Lord Jesus and the key to a peaceful life was confession. The vehicle that takes me from Glory to Glory is humility.

I remember my childhood very clearly. I was a well-kept child, a spoiled child, never been deprived of any material thing. I was sheltered from the world for a time. Just as an unborn baby, I was kept in a protective sac at the center of the whole world. Then one day something happened to cause me to notice that it wasn't just me in my world. There was this woman that I adored. My mother! Although my father was completely out of my life, I felt as though I had everything. You really don't miss what you've never had and that was my belief system at a very young age. I learned later on that biological parents should both be present or something will be void in the child. I grew up and started dating older guys. I know now that I was looking for something that could only come from your dad. So when I met Jesus, he introduced me to my Father in Heaven.

I remember my relationships with other kids. I liked having the company, I was lonely. By me being an only child, and a protected one, I was so naive. I started early, people pleasing. I would do anything for a friend. I learned things from other kids, but not very well. I would always be the one who got caught and got caught up. Looking back I see that some of my first relationships set me on a path to a destination called hell. Lying, Cheating, Stealing and sexual experimentation were learned behaviors and by the time I was old enough to know better I was well on the path that lead to my destruction.

I rarely got punished or spanked, but when I did it was always because of some of my unperfected techniques that I learned from my peers. No, I was not perfect, but what other kids showed me to do, I would do them and get caught. They seemed to have left out the part about how to conceal it. That always broke my heart and I knew that this *wonderful world* was not as wonderful as it had seemed. I met the other side and as much as I tried to avoid reality, there reality was kicking my behind again. I remember getting excellent grades in school. I was an achiever. I found out later on that this is what was expected of me and I had to please people. This wasn't very hard in the setting that I was in, but then the setting changed.

My mother got married when I was seven years old. I remember feeling a little remorse. Until then, I had my mommy to myself. But truly, I was glad to be gaining a dad. We moved into a house with his sister and her child and everything changed. Everything! My mom was happy in her new marriage, I could tell. She had the glow she used to have before my biological father got married to someone else when I was a toddler. I was happy for her; I loved her so very much. I wasn't too particular about him or his family, but she was always able to make me feel all right. I found out that she could make everybody feel all right. It was very clear to me later on where my people pleasing technique came from.

The Holy Ghost told me that this book is not to expose other people, but to expose the spirits within them and within myself. My new cousin and I lived together, and as much as I wanted a sister, we never really got along. She and her mother stayed in the basement and my mom would always invite her to stay upstairs with me over night. She and I would sleep together and we experimented with sex often. At this early age a lesbian spirit had attached itself to me.

One day they moved out and I was forced to deal with loneliness and the fact that my mom was married and I didn't come first anymore. But she was so good at covering up until she had convinced me to believe that everything was going to work out. My cousin's friends became my so-called friends. The more my mom cleaved to her husband, I cleaved to my newfound friends. I went to school outside of the neighborhood, so when I got to go outside, all we did in our recreation was fight. Fighting was new, something that I did not like and did not want a part of. Nor was I very good at it. But, I soon learned.

My grandfather and I were very close. He got tired of me coming home crying because someone was picking on me, I took a martial arts class and everyday it seemed that I had to prove myself. I had a friend who was somewhat like me, she people- pleased. We got along very well until someone else came around. She would bring her friends home from school to fight me. I was fooled because when we were alone, we did the lesbian thing. I found out early on that this was one way to please people. I also discovered betrayal.

One day I looked around to see that my friend has grown up and I mean she was grown, like overnight and I wondered what was wrong with her that she didn't want to play anymore, we were about twelve or thirteen and she had a boyfriend. He had a car and she would get me to walk with her to the store to meet him. I thought this was so exciting; I had to get a boyfriend, too. I met a guy who also went to school outside of the neighborhood and we were in the same boat; we were the outsiders. All we would do is talk on the phone for almost a year. One day while my mother was at choir rehearsal, he came over and I met him in the back yard and we kissed. I thought that kiss was the best thing to ever happen to me. He passed out on the porch so I figured that it was the best thing to happen to him, too. I was attending a school across town and there I met another boyfriend, and this guy was sexually active, but I was a virgin. The group of girls that I went to school with and the group of boys from school would hang out together and do social things like movies, go to McDonald's, to the Inner Harbor. But, I still had this other group of friends from home that did otherwise. One day I was in class and my boyfriend was walking down the hall and he looked into the classroom and called me a virgin. I thought that was the worst thing in the world to be called. Peer pressure set in and I had my mind set on losing my virginity. I had this boyfriend at school and this boyfriend from the neighborhood, but I did not sleep with either of them. I asked my girlfriend to set me up with one of her friend's friends. He had a car and there we were. We had something in common again. I slept with this man he was twenty-one and I was fourteen.

I believed that sex would feel like it did with girls. I never knew that something could hurt so badly. When he finished using me, he dropped me off on the basketball court and everyone knew that this man had been with me. I remember then, wishing that I could go back to the day that someone called me "virgin."

Around this time I found out that my mom was pregnant and I was delighted. My momma was having a baby! So this was a new thing to be excited about, I was going to be a big sister. I came home from school one day and being the woman that I thought I was, I wanted to surprise my mother with dinner, so I stewed some chicken and I added some noodles. My stepfather came home and he screamed at me for cooking this pot of chicken. It later dawned on me that when my mom stewed chicken she would cook two pots, one with noodles and one with rice. He told me that he would make me eat the whole pot. I was devastated. This was the first time this man ever raised his voice at me. The hitting started very shortly after. I was heartbroken because my mom did not believe me nor did she protect me. She chose him!

Everyday mom and I were being separated more and more, and I gravitated to the things in the street. I was learning how to smoke cigarettes and marijuana with my cousins at the time. Everything that would cover up the loneliness, abandonment and betrayal that I felt, I would try it. That was the beginning of my end. I had turned fifteen years old and we were about to move into a new house. My mother let my new boyfriend come over once and then she started doing funny things like telling me to ask my stepfather if he could come. She had completely lost her mind. It seemed as though now that he was to become a father he wanted to practice on me.

When I saw that they were standing together against me, I rebelled against both of them. I even tried fighting back. That just made everything worst! I was a kid and I couldn't win and I couldn't make anyone believe what was going on. When my mother was there he was verbally and mentally abusive and when she was not, he would fight me.

My sister was born and we moved into the new house. These were truly the worst days of my life. I was away from my friends and in the process of changing schools. We had no phone and I could not contact my boyfriend.

On a Saturday afternoon my aunt and cousin came over and I was so glad to have company. I went over to their house. When we got there we were getting our hair done and the phone rang. It was my cousin's boyfriend. He was coming over to see her and she asked him to bring a friend. When they arrived I went downstairs to take a peek at the friend. Much to my surprise, I saw my boyfriend standing in her living room. I knew my life was over then. Everything went so terribly wrong and of course I blamed my stepfather for not letting me date. This was my first experience with feeling less than. Her breast was bigger, she was prettier and he chose her and that was all of the evidence I needed to start the process of hating myself. It seemed like forever before I would start school again. When I did, I was glad because there is nothing like a fresh start. Those hours away from my stepfather was longed for.

I met a new guy in school and he was so nice looking and he really liked me. I remember brushing him off at first because I felt that I wasn't pretty enough. This guy really liked me and we became young lovers. This was the first real boyfriend that I'd ever had. One day his sister introduced him to a girl and she was so beautiful. I found out that he was seeing her and immediately, I excused myself from the relationship. I felt that I was less than she and that he would love her. That wasn't true for him. He didn't even really like her. Their relationship was short. He called and asked me to go with his sister and her boyfriend to the park. I told him yes, but when they showed up this new girl was there. I couldn't see that he was all over me, and not really paying her any attention. I just focused on what she was and what I was not. After that day I broke up with him just because I was insecure. That's what happens when someone beats you. You start to feel like nothing.

I had an uncle named Robbie. He and his wife, Momma Selma, took care of me while my mom worked when I was younger. This bond was not easily broken. I loved the whole family. One Sunday we were in Church and my uncle asked me when was I going to be saved and he explained salvation to me. I told him that my mom was going to have a baby. He heard me, but he went right back to talking about Jesus. He was concerned about my salvation.

That night, after church, I had a dream. We lived near the graveyard so the graveyard was a part of my dream. I dreamed that Momma Selma, was dead and she was sitting on our living room sofa. Her head was resting on her hand. When her head fell over, she'd pick it back up and rest it on her hand again. I remember that seeming very strange to me and I was scared of her. At the time, my grandmother was sitting in the dining room in front of the window. She said, "Come here. Do you want to know what it feels like to have a spirit go through your body?" I answered yes and went to her, laid my body across her lap and felt something go through me. It felt like ice. Then the doorbell woke me up. My Mom went to the door and it was my other grand mom bearing the news. My Uncle Robbie had passed away. This was my first experience with death. Also, to the best of my memory, this was around the time that I found out that I had visions.

I remember a dream I had when I was fifteen. I dreamed that I had come home from school and my stepfather told me that my mom was dead. I cried so pitiful. I couldn't believe that she had left me with him. I went in their room and lay on the bed and cried. "God just give me one more minute with her, please, God, I want to tell her that I love her." Just then I heard her in the kitchen cooking for her own wake and I went in the kitchen to her. "Ma! Come here." There were people in the kitchen with her so I pulled her outside by the driveway. I started complaining, "how could you leave me with him, you know he hates me. How could you leave without saying good-bye."? I just carried on. She started looking really faint and jumped into the trashcan. That thing tore me up. I was scared to look in the trashcan so I just banged on the top of it. A securi ty guard came from the back yard and told me that there is no one in the trashcan. I watched him walk out of sight and then I took off the lid and there my mom was, in pieces.

When I woke up, and I know I was woke, something told me to turn on the radio and to turn it up very loud. I didn't know if she was alive or dead, but if she was alive she would run in this room and tell me to turn it down. A voice came from the radio and said, "If you want to see your mother again, call her three times." My voice was so faint the first time, "Ma," I whispered. The other two times I screamed for her with everything in me. "Maaaaaa, Mommieeeeeee." She came through the door with a flowing nightgown and she wasn't wearing her glasses. I sat back up on the bed and I told her to stay away for I knew that she was a ghost. I couldn't go to school that day and I couldn't go past the driveway. I was terrified. That dream took so much out of me. It would be fifteen more years before I knew exactly what that vision meant.

Chapter Three

LOOKING BACK

As time went on, my home situation got worse and worse. My stepfather would continue to fight me. I would try to tell my grandparents, but they wouldn't listen. I even tried to call my real father and he asked me "What did you do"? Very typical thinking from a person with little information. I was made to feel as though I deserved to be beaten.

My family took me to the family psychiatrist. He talked to my mother and stepfather first. When it was my time to go into his office, he started telling me that I would be grown soon and that I would go on to live my life, so therefore, don't mess up your mother's relationship. I felt that the weight of the world was placed on my shoulders. I felt responsible for the fact that I was not this man's child and that he did not like me. I was made to feel that the beatings were my fault. I was really starting to believe that I was inadequate and I became more insecure.

Looking back on these things is very painful. "Jesus, must I continue?" I was just a kid and things were already at the worst, I thought. Jesus told me that I had to continue, for weeping may endure for a night, but joy cometh in the morning. Little did I know, this was going to be one very long night. I would say nightmare but I was very much awake and very much a participant.

One day while mother was at work, my baby sister wet my bed so I was asleep on the living room chair. My stepfather came in and told me to move. I made up in my mind that I would fight back if he ever touched me again, but I found myself explaining that my bed was wet. He didn't care he. He and I got to fighting and two of my teeth were knocked out. He called my mother and told her to come home. She did not come right away, but his sister showed up, she told him that he was wrong. That was the first time someone had ever stood up for me. When my mother came home I remember standing in the door with my teeth in my hand and she walked right past me and asked him what happened. That day I ran away for a couple of hours. When I returned I told my mother that I was going to call the police on him and she told me that they would only take me away. I remember thinking how terribly hopeless I felt. From that day on, I didn't believe in justice and I felt that no one was on my side.

I felt so insecure about my teeth. Here I was seventeen and already I had some sort of denture in my mouth. I was very good in school, probably because I loved to be there. I wasn't the type of girl that boys would pick up. Sol started picking up boys. I fell in love with a boy from my chemistry class who later would become my husband. We did everything together and he was the one person that I felt was on my side. We were very much in love. He appeared to be so strong and I depended on that strength.

My fiancee' decided that he would join the Marine Corp when he graduated and I was convinced that I could not live without him. The day before he left for boot camp, he was at my house. We were in the basement watching TV. All of a sudden we heard this Boom so I ran up the steps to see what had fallen. I reached the top of the stairs and I saw my stepfather holding my mother down. I remember the look on her face. He had never done this before. I screamed, "Momma, I told you he was like this." I was cursing him out and he acted like he was coming for me. I remember thinking that if I was to hit him and he let my mother go, would she then protect me. I came to the conclusion that she never protected me before.

By this time my boyfriend was at the top of the stairs and he told my stepfather not to hit me. I ran out of the house and my boyfriend came behind me. I felt that he was my prince on a white horse because he came to my rescue. We had planned to get married. Even though I felt that he loved me, what I realized later is that my stepfather gave him the message that it was all right to beat your wife and he listened.

During my senior year I only needed two credits so I went to night school. I was home during the day, directly in harms way with my stepfather and we really did fight then. I had a cousin named Tammy who was a foster child. I really loved her. I had started going to Cosmetology school and she would let me practice on her hair. One morning the doorbell rang and it woke me up. It was Tammy, and my stepfather let her in. She came in and told me that she was going to get some money and what she wanted done to her hair. She had been there for about ten minutes and he came in the room and asked her to leave. I couldn't believe my ears. He let her in and then put her out. She wasn't a model person, but I never looked down on Tammy. It hurt me to see someone treat her badly.

She left in peace, but after she left he told me that he did not want her in his house. I asked him why he let her in then. There was a big fight. I knew what the word hate meant. I had no peace. My boyfriend was gone and I was so alone. My mom was split in half. I think she knew now what was going on, but she had this baby and surely she didn't want to raise another child alone.

My mother was trapped, I was trapped and I felt that the only way out was to marry. In 1984, I graduated from high school, Cosmetology school and got married. What a remarkable year of accomplishment. What a setup!

Chapter Four

"I DO"

On my wedding day a girlfriend of my husband's put something in his hand while we were in the receiving line. It was two vials of cocaine. Then for a time he was missing. We left and went to my mother's house for a reception. On our honeymoon, my husband dropped the bornb. I could not go back with him to California unless he had a car. We were on the car lot that night looking and with our monitory wedding gifts, we got a car.

Three days on the road to California and on the third day I was convinced that I had made the biggest mistake of my life. We stopped in New Mexico to eat. I walked up and down the mall trying to find a menu that I understood. There were no familiar places to eat. So my husband told me to eat some of his strange food. When I didn't, he told me that I'd better eat then because he wasn't going to stop anymore. My fairy tale was over.

When we got our first apartment we were really roughing it. We went to a garage sale and got a recliner, a yellow and white polka dot chair, and a little coffee table. I figured everything would be all right. One day he asked me for my receipts from hair school. I asked him why. He wanted to file them on his taxes. My mother put me through hair school, why did he feel like he had the right to claim her money? He showed me why he felt like he had the right. I was his property or much less. People don't treat their property like he treated me. I thought like most battered women, like this would be the only time he hit me, like I could change him. Then I started believing that it was all my fault. But, I loved him. It seemed that I loved him more with each fight.

We went to K-Mart one day and a young lady told me that she liked my hair. Needless to say that I was feeling a little below safe self esteem level, I was surprised. I told her that I was a hair stylist and she became my biggest customer. She was my only customer and my only friend in California. I was so glad that I had someone to talk to finally. Corina and I got along very well. Even though we had so much in common, our lives and our perspectives were quite different. She came from an abusive home as well. She was married to a Marine, like I was. But Corina had the confidence of a queen. She worked at the mall and she had so many pretty clothes. Me doing her hair would put the icing on the cake. She was Sharp! Corina's husband was about to go overseas and she seemed so happy. That's when I met her friend Ike. Ike was a white officer and he lined her pockets real good. I was beginning to wonder where all of the fine clothes, the Audi, the nice furniture and all of the money came from. She told me after one of my episodes with my husband that it hurt her to see me with a black man. Shocked at her comment, I stopped crying and started to laugh.

My husband, Wayne and I went shopping another day and got me a pet. His name was Sam Edward Raye Burke. This was the smartest creature that I had ever seen. Wayne named him Houdini. This hamster could get out of anything. We brought a cage a week. We couldn't afford one of the nicer ones. We would place him in his cage and place books on top of the cage. He would chew through the top of the cage and then through the books. One day, Wayne put a Bible on top of his cage and he ate a hole right through the word of God. When he got out we could hear him under the baseboards around the kitchen. He would get lost and we would find him, catch him and put him back. During the day when Wayne was at work, I would place him on the table and pour out a bag of Sunflower seeds. Believe me, there was not much more to eat most of the time. I depended on Sam's company. I talked to him when no one else would listen. Many times the phone was off and I couldn't talk to my family unless I went to the pay phone. Things weren't that great, but when Wayne was home I felt like I had everything. As bad as everything was, I found out that my husband should have allotted me some money every pay. This went towards the new car that I never got to drive.

Corina alerted me to things like that. Now that her husband was overseas she spent most of her time with Ike. I hardly got to see her. Then one day she came to get me and took me to his condo. This was their love nest and he gave her the money to decorate it. Her taste was impeccable. The burgundy and mahogany wood color scheme gave the whole place a look of luxury. The leather furniture and the plush carpet, the huge bed that they had with the wooden canopy and the lighted headboard. Man this was living. I started to believe that she meant what she said to me about being with a black man. Every time I was with her I felt alive. I felt like anything was possible, I dreamed of how things would be one day when my husband and I were on our feet.

One Sunday afternoon I waited for my husband to come home and I waited, and I waited. No sign of Wayne anywhere. I was worried. When he came home it was almost morning. I looked so ugly. My eyes were swollen from crying all night. With me still being a kid, I hadn't developed the art of crying silently. I was hoarse and my hair was a mess. "Where have you been?" Oh he would come up with stories as long as the coast of California. I don't remember the story that he told that time, but I found out that it was a lie. The next day he was trying to be so nice. He let me drive the car to the store. Me being suspicious, I searched the car. Under the casing of the emergency break I found a number. "Rose!" When I got home I asked him about Rose and he tried to kill me. He hated being caught in a lie and this would cause me most of my beatings.

Corina took me to the hospital that night and my arm was fractured. I made up in my mind as I called my family from the emergency room that I was going home for good. But it would be a few days before I could get a flight. I packed the next morning after he had gone to work. It took me longer with the cast on my arm. When he came home he caught me packing. I was down on my knees in the closet. He grabbed me by the back of my head and told me that I wasn't going anywhere. He pulled me back up on the bed between his legs and squeezed as hard as he could. We both thought that I was pregnant. He told me that I wasn't leaving with his baby. I was in so much pain from the fight a day before. My arm fractured, my eyes black and now my stomach was cramping beyond belief.

As usual after the fight he went out and I called Corina to come and get me. I told her that I would stay with her until I was able to go home. I loaded everything into her car and Sam into my coat pocket. Once we reached Corina's house, I loaded my stuff onto the curb so that she could park the car. "Sam" I shouted. "Don't tell me you brought that rat with you," Corina said with a look of horror on her face. She thought that Sam had gotten out in her car. For real I don't know where Sam got out. I was already upset about the ordeal, but now I had lost my Sam. I sat up with Corina for a long time talking as she tried to convince me to stay in California and get a job. I told Corina I wanted to go home. I was a baby and though things were terrible back home, at least I could eat. Corina told me, as she yarned "Tammy don't go back to that man." Immediately I rebelled. I thought who was she to tell me that I couldn't go back to him. After all, he was my husband. I left my things and I started back to the apartment to try to make things work with Wayne.

Corina lived a long, long way from me, at least walking and it took me hours to reach home, but I was determined. Plus, Corina would curse me out if I called her and told her to come get me at my halfway point. So I swung that cast and I walked and I walked. Once I reached the complex I could see the rising of the California sun. It was so beautiful. I didn't have my key so I knocked at the front door. I was knocking for about twenty minutes waking up the neighbors. They wanted to call, but we didn't have a phone. I thought that my husband had gotten bold and had a woman in the house. I went around to the bedroom window, which was maybe two feet from the grass, and I knocked. He came to the window and opened it. I climbed through the narrow window with my cast as he returned to his nap. I joined him. Damn, I was tired. I had water in my eyes later that morning as I told him that I had lost Sam. He didn't seem to care at all. He often reminded me of how much of a child I was.

That afternoon after a long conversation with self, I decided that I would still go home. Grandma and her Choice Card were coming through for me again. I pulled myself together and did my hair. I went to the payphone to confirm that the flight reservation was made. While holding the phone, a man walked past me and smiled. He walked up the stairs in front of me and he looked over the balcony and asked me "What happened to your arm?" I signaled to him with my fist to answer his question. He then asked if I would like to talk about it. I told him yes. After I got off of the phone I went up to his place and we began to talk. "My name is Casper," he said. I thought, "I know that's right." He looked like a little black ghost, but his personality was golden and true. I told him of how my husband was cheating and that when he was caught he liked to fight. He was such a good listener. He didn't try to come on to me in any way. He lived in the house with two other guys, Chuck, a big guy from DC, which was right next door to my home in Baltimore, and Carl. Fine, Fine, Fine! Carl was from the south and he had this cute accent, a gold tooth that made me feel right at home and he could dance so well. This was my first thought of having any other man.

As I sat there in their living room giving up less and less information there was a knock at the door. Chuck opened the door without even looking out. "Hey, Rose." Immediately my heart dropped. I had a million thoughts going through my mind at that time. What was she doing here? Damn, she's just the neighborhood freak, isn't she? I would kick her butt with my one arm. Two very young Philippine girls walked into the living room. "Tammy, this is Rose and Rose." I didn't say a word. I just listened as one of them started to pour out her heart. "My mom put me out. I stayed out all night the other night and she told me I had to leave." She said that her mother is sending her back to her country. "I don't want to go back there. Can I stay here?" It was the ugly one that made me feel much better as I sat there with my blackened eyes. I recognized her voice from the other day when my neighbor Rachelle and I called her house. Her mom told her to get off the phone, that she had to go to school. I asked her how old she was and she said that she was fourteen. That was what my husband and I were fighting about. Not only was he out all night with this chick, she was a baby. I told him that he would go to jail. Now here she was before me and I knew that out of the two Rose's, I had picked the right one. "You stayed out all night with my husband, you b___! I ought to whip your butt." I had forgotten all about my arm being restricted. Casper jumped in between us. "Tammy, she just got put out of her house. She's just a child." And he was right. I felt compassionate as I listened to her ramble.

I told Rose to walk with me and we talked. She told me that nothing had happened that night, but he had tried all night to sleep with her. I hung on to every word, as I wanted every detail. Then she told me that she was still a virgin. "A Virgin?" I asked. She said yes. She was so seductive to be so ugly with her deep voice and slurred speech with broken English. Somehow I began to like Rose. She told me out of concern; "Maybe you and Wayne should have a baby, that would make things better." I answered her foolish suggestion swiftly. "It doesn't work like that in this country. If it isn't working, a baby won't change anything." I thought that maybe Wayne had mentioned to her that he wanted a child. But at the time we thought that I may be pregnant, why was he with her? I asked her why she was going to stay in the house with three men if she was so much of a virgin. I had a genuine concern for the kid who had almost stolen my husband. "Why don't you come home with me?" She agreed.

Wayne came in the house and the first thing he saw was Rose standing on top of the chair screaming, "dat mush be dat shing zuu looking fo!" Sam ran across the floor and you could have brought Wayne for two cents. He told me that I was crazy for bringing her there. He turned around and spun back out the door. I was so glad to see Sam and he was glad to see me. I didn't even have to chase him. He ran and jumped up into my hand. I was thinking that the last time I noticed Sam moving in my coat pocket was in Corina's car on the way to her house. I thought to myself, "This is one smart rat." Nevertheless, he found his way back home to me. Rose and I had a lovely evening. We talked and talked some more. I played some music for her and watched her dance. I wanted to be with her and I found myself thinking as she did her thing, "Now I see why Wayne wanted her."

My Lesbian issues were starting to resurface. The only thing that kept me from acting out on that was the fact that she was fourteen. I could see me and my husband in jail for rape. She took a bath and I gave her one of my nighties to sleep in. We ate some dinner and went to bed. I had put to rest any idea of being with this kid. She was like a little sister. So naive and so trusting. In the middle of the night Wayne came home and did everything to try and wake her up. He took a shower, poured on triple portions of his favorite cologne and had a towel wrapped around his waste. I knew what he was thinking. I knew he thought that we had been together; especially when I told him that we are suppose to share everything. I never told him any different.

The next morning we woke up. He and I had slept on the living room floor giving our bed to our houseguest. He asked me "are you still going home today"? "Yes, I said, but first I want you to take Rose to school." He looked at me as if to question my sincerity. "You got her put out of her house Wayne so I guess she'll have to live here with you."

When Rose woke up, I had given her an outfit to put on and a raincoat to where to school. I curled her hair and she swore that her hair had never been curled in her life. She was so grateful. I told Rose that I was leaving and to take care of herself. She was going out the door behind my husband. They took a long, long time. I knew I couldn't take Sam with me so I asked this little kid that looked just like Emanuel Lewis to take Sam. He asked his mother and she agreed. At this point all I could think about was going home and crying on my grandma's shoulder. She could believe that this man beat me, but she never believed that my stepfather did too. I loved the validation and the special attention. I had missed my plane, but I went to the airport and waited as a standby. A few hours later it was time to go home.

When I stepped off the plane, my baby sister and my mom were there to greet me. I was so glad to see them. I forgot that my face had been distorted, but I was reminded by the look on their faces. I had lost weight and they said that I was white as a ghost. I enjoyed being home with them. I felt safe. I didn't fear that Edward would hit me again and if he did I would kill him. After I had layed down to sleep that night, I couldn't believe that I had left my husband and I wanted to go back to him that moment, just like the night when I left Corina's. I was three thousand miles away and I couldn't swim. About a week later after moping around and running up my families phone bill talking to my husband, I had talked to Rachelle, my neighbor, the one who knew about Rose. She told me that Rose was knocking at my door one morning. She said that Wayne opened the door, but Rose never went in. She was perplexed. She said that Rose handed him a bag. "Oh, maybe she was returning my clothes" I explained. "Your clothes?" She replied like someone had blown her over with a strong wind. "Yes" I told her that I had let Rose stay over and she couldn't hold back the laughter. She said that I was a trip.

My grandmother told me that I could go back if I wanted to. I went right back to my husband. I found out later about having a dependency for not only substance, but having a dependency for people. In other words, obsession. This was my second experience with "Obsession," and his cousin "Compulsion," was not too far behind. I would get beat up, come home and fly right back to him. I really believed that I was nothing without him, but I couldn't be anything with him. The pain was so great and after the bruises were no longer visible to your eyes, I could still see them and feel them. I would cry all night sometimes. This is where I must have picked up on the idea that I was the victim. Jesus revealed to me later that a lot of times I volunteered.

When I went back to be with my husband I told myself that I would make this work. I couldn't work in a California salon because I didn't have my license and I needed another 500 hours of training to qualify in that state. Things went well for about a month. Then the fights started all over again. My husband stayed out whenever he wanted to. I spent all day watching soaps and my nights were full of tears. Sometimes I would call home and get my parents to send me money. I would have the money in time to fix dinner for my husband. Sometimes he wouldn't show and other times he would start a fight about where the money came from. He actually thought that I was sleeping with someone for the money. At this point it didn't sound like a bad idea. He started working a second job delivering pizzas at night. Me, I had gotten quite used to going to see Casper, Chuck and Carl. We had become really good friends. I had finally found a job at Arby's. I would steal food to eat. One day I worked all day and Wayne didn't pick me up from work. I had to walk home. Still he didn't show up that night at all. This was the first time that I really believed that something had happened to him. I was very upset. The next day when he came home, he had another great story. Glad that he was alive, I believed him.

I woke one morning to find that my husband wasn't feeling well. He was camped out on the chair in the living room. I left my keys on the table and went to do a young lady's hair for her prom. When I returned, my husband was gone. So I went out to the parking lot to see if I saw his car. I didn't. Just then a car pulled up beside me. It was my favorite three friends, Casper, Chuck and Carl. "Tammy, Old boy ain't shit. Old Boy ain't shit." "What are you talking about "? I asked. Don't your husband drive the white Mitsubishi? Got fox on the front? "Ummmm Hmmmm," I replied wondering what kind of news they had for me. I thought that maybe he knew that I would go over their house and had approached them or something. No, this was not the case. My husband had so much dirt going on at the time until he didn't even notice, nor did he care if I was to sleep around. I was starting to think about it. Trust me. Every time I saw that Carl, I wanted to melt. "We just saw old boy at the pier. He was all up on this Mexican girl, kissing her on the boardwalk." My eyes started to leak. They continued. "He has on some gray sweatpants with stars going down the leg and a white tee shirt. I know that was old boy." I went back over to my customer's house and waited for a time. Hard to hold back the tears, I couldn't help but break in Hazel's arms. Hazel was a middle aged black woman. She drove the bus for a living. Her daughter was going to her senior prom that night. She knew I was having a hard time and since I had lost contact with Corina, I would go over to her house to talk to her. She was so supportive and she treated me like I was one of her girls. I told her that I would be back. I would normally cut through the complex, but this time I went back through the parking lot to see if I saw Wayne's car. He was coming up the parking lot blasting his favorite Fat Boys tape. He pulled up next to me and I asked him where he had been. He parked the car and got out. We went into the house as I am chattering away at him "You know I didn't have my keys." "Oh I'm sorry," he said "I just went to the store." I watched as he made a trip to the store turn into one of his great adventures, noticing that he had on exactly what the 3C's had told me. I asked him about the woman at the pier with the white and black shirt on and his whole attitude changed. Now, he would turn this around. It was always "who told you that"? I told him that that didn't matter, but it did. That was the most important thing to my husband. Knowing who snitched on him this time. When I didn't tell, he beat the hell out of me that day.

I had no intentions on telling him about the 3 C's (Casper, Chuck and Carl), but by the end of that whipping I would have told on anyone to get him off me. And, I thought that just maybe, they would get him off of me. I stood there at their door messed up. Finally Chuck came to the door. "Baby Girl!" He looked at my husband like what the hell was he doing at their door. I asked Chuck with the little breath I had left to please tell my husband what he had told me earlier. Chuck told Wayne. "Yeah man, I saw you earlier today with that chick, down on the pier, kissing." Wayne looked at this dude and asked, "You wanna f**k my wife? Chuck told him that if he didn't stop messing around that someone's going to have me. I noticed that all of my husband's courage went away as Carl and Casper joined Chuck to see what the problem was. "Damn girl what's wrong with your eye?"

Wayne turned with the quickness to go back to the apartment. I followed him, thinking I gave him what he wanted. I turned in my friend. I was wondering why he was mad at me and I had forgotten that I was supposed to be mad at him. I followed him back into the apartment where he commenced to beating me up. My neighbor had called the police. When the police knocked on the door, I told him that we were fighting and he told Wayne that he had to leave for a few hours. I asked the police could he just get me to the airport. He told me that that wasn't within his jurisdiction. That he couldn't go that far. He offered a ride to the hospital, but I continued to beg, explaining, "He's going to kill me." I was beaten pretty badly; I remember barely making it on the plane. While sitting there the stewardess asked me if I was ok and if I wanted a drink. I told her no.

When I got back home my mother and grandparents were so upset. My grandmother gave me a little pink pill. That pill knocked me out. I woke up wondering how in hell I got back there so quickly. I was clearly having a nervous breakdown. One afternoon I was at my mother's house taking a bath. She opened the door as I dried off and she screamed, looking at my bruises from head to toe. She cried. That is when I realized how badly I had been beaten. My family managed to talk me into sticking around this time. I went ahead and got my cosmetology license. Then, months later I was talking to my husband again. He wasn't even telling me to come home this time. Which made me want to go out there and see what was going on.

One day Wayne called me and told me that he had been restricted to the base for smoking marijuana and that he had lost a stripe. He told me that some girl had gotten on the base and keyed his car. I felt so bad for him and I wanted to be with him. Once he was off of restriction, he called and told me that I could come home.

Chapter Five

INSANITY

I heard in a twelve-step program once, that insanity is doing the same things and expecting different results. I was the same old Tammy and my husband was very much himself when I decided to return.

I met Wayne at the LAX. He had another couple with him. Antwan and Janet. We all went out to dinner and then retired to one of the base housing units. We sat there and drank and smoked pot for hours. I remember entertaining them with the newest east coast dance to the newest Doug E. Fresh song. They were fun. I was tired and I was wondering when we would be going home. That's when Wayne told me that we did not have a home. That we'd be staying there until we got a place. We stayed in the kid's room on a cot.

The next morning, I continued to probe. "Where are all of our things?" The bed, TV, recliner and my yellow polka dot chair wasn't much. But they did make life a little easier. With me running back and forth, consistency was comforting. He told me that the things were in storage. He went and got the t.v. in the morning and some dishes. The following day when he went to work, I got a chance to meet Janet's friends. I was fully aware of the lifestyles on the base. How they swapped husbands and wives and I knew that Wayne had slept with every one of them. They were in the living room talking about their children and their labor. "How was your labor, Tammy? Burke told us that you had a baby young." "Oh, it was o.k." What was I saying? What the hell were they talking about? I didn't have a baby. Later I asked him about it and he told me that in order to get more money that he told them that we had a kid. He was flashing around pictures of my baby sister and our life was a big lie.

Janet was a lot of fun, even though I knew that she was tired of me being in her house. She and her husband fought worse than Wayne and I but I loved the fact that she would never get beat up. She was a strong-minded black sister from Chicago and she called cigarettes squares. She took no crap off of Antwan. One night my husband left me the car. Could you believe that? I went to the store that night to get Janet some pain medicine for her tooth and some "Squares." I wasn't supposed to be gone long; we were in the middle of a game of Rummy 5000. "Can I have two packs of Newport 100, and some Tylenol?" The attendant reached for the cigarettes as he explained, "We don't sell medicines."

When I was pulling away from the parking lot, I heard someone shouting "Burke, Burke!" Someone thought that it was my husband. I stopped to see what they wanted and a man stepped from the car. "Oh, hi Tammy, welcome back." He already knew too much. How did he know that I left? My husband introduced me to this guy once, his name was Wayne also. We began to talk. He asked me how I liked living in our apartment. I advised that we are living with friends in Sterling Homes. He was amazed and it was clear that this was yet another lie that my husband had told. His motive was probably money again.

Wayne talked to me for hours as the mysteries unfolded. He told me about the girl who scratched up his car. He told me that was where our furniture was and that we couldn't get it all back because her husband was back from overseas. He explained that we didn't lose the apartment. My husband gave it up to play house with the woman and her kids while her husband was away. He amazed me with how much he knew. He told me that we had a daughter. I stepped out of the car with my slim self, weighing about 98 lbs. I asked him "Does it look like I had a baby?" Showing off my little petite figure, my bad east coast haircut. He said no as his face had the expression that told me he liked what he saw. By this time I was so nervous. My legs were shaking and I was wondering how I would drive home and how would I approach my husband with this. But there was more. He told me the date that my flight came in. How did he know this? He told me that I was supposed to come that Friday, which was true. I explained that my husband couldn't get a flight that day. He told me that my husband had the flight and postponed it so that he could be with this other lady. So he knew everything. I asked him to help me get my things and he did.

Antwan helped me to get my things into the house. Wayne was nowhere around. He had done his part and he didn't want any trouble out of Chi-town and B-more. Wayne and Antwan had names for themselves. After we unloaded the bed, which was on top of the car and the little things that I managed to fit inside and in the trunk, Antwan left. I struggled to fit everything in and I planned what I would say on the drive to base in the morning when I picked up Wayne. I was going to tell him that I loved him, and let's put the past behind us.

That was not the way it went down. I woke up that morning by the slamming of the front door. My husband came into the room with all of his field gear on. He told me "By the time I get these clothes off, you'd better tell me who you've been talking to from my job." I was caught off guard. "Baby don't worry about it, we got our things back." Again he said, "You're going to tell me who on my job told you this shit." Antwan had gone straight to Wayne and told him that I had gotten our furniture back and that I was upset. But, as usual, my husband made it seem like I had done something so wrong. He turned it around again and I knew that I was about to get another beating.

He sat on me with his fat butt and his thick thighs and pinned me down. He slapped me in my face over and over all day long and no one would help me. No one. I endured hours of his torture, when a commercial came on the t.v. "He has a car like that." "On my job? No way!" "Yes and he has the same name as you." He jumped off of me and I ran to the bathroom to assess the damage. Antwan and Janet stayed completely out of it. No one would ever help me out, I thought. I left the unit to go to the store. I called my grandma and she told me that I would have to stay this time, and I understood. She had flown me back twice. So I called the number that Wayne had given me and he told me that when he had to leave that he was going back to Georgia and that I could ride that far with him. He told me to save flight money so that I could get a flight home from there.

I had no choice but to stay this time. I tried to make it work. I knew that I had better not ever mention what I heard to my husband again. I promised myself that I would be the good wife until I was able to get back home. One day I had found a phone number and asked my husband about it. Sometimes, I couldn't resist. I asked him about it and we argued. Janet heard him tell me that this was Antwan's number and they began to fight. I felt better. I won't lie. Misery sure does love company. That goes for my husband too, who was bringing Antwan down with him. We had no kids, but they had two kids. That was just one of the fights between Antwan and Janet.

One night Antwan had stayed out all night. Wayne came home and acted as if nothing was wrong. Janet questioned him over and over about the whereabouts of her husband. Wayne just kept lying telling her that he didn't know where Antwan was. So later that evening we were sitting in the dining area when we heard a key in the door. Janet had locked the top lock and Antwan was trying to get in. She lined up the can goods on the table. "Hold up Burke, don't open that damned door" she shouted as Wayne reached for the lock to let Antwan in. After she had unloaded the whole cabinet she looked at Wayne and told him, "O.K. let him in." She threw every one of the canned goods at Antwan before he could even get to her. I enjoyed it. I had never seen a woman fight back like this. Wayne was laughing and Antwan laughed as well, even though it was evident that he was highly embarrassed. He wore a mask for my husband and I. When he got his hands on Janet he threw her out of the house. Janet immediately called the Military Police and we were escorted out. There was not supposed to be two families living in a unit.

So there we were with nowhere to live. I thought my husband would be generous and send me back home, but he told me when I picked him up from work the next day that we were going to stay with some friends. That's when I met Debbie and Donnell. They lived in a small town on the other side of the base called San Clemente. That was such a beautiful little town. It sat right on the beach. Debbie worked at Kentucky Friend Chicken and every night she brought home free chicken. She had a six-month-old baby. They were a really nice young couple. They stayed in a studio apartment and it was needless to say that we crowded it rather quickly. We slept in their living room. Things seemed like they were going well. I kept the baby while Debbie worked.

Sometimes in the evening Donnell would invite his boys over and I would go into their bedroom and watch television. Wayne claimed to be in the field almost every other week Debbie was starting to get a little tired of us being there and Wayne hadn't given her one-dime since we started living there. I didn't care as long as he and I were getting along. And, we were until one payday. My husband did not come home. He hadn't come home for two days. I felt pressure from Debbie as I had to depend on her for a meal and Donnell had gotten really comfortable with inviting his friends over. I was so upset. I didn 't know if Wayne was o.k. or not, but Donnell seemed to know where he was. I decided to take a walk to the beach. I was so uncomfortable in the house and without Wayne it was horrible. I walked down the street avoiding the homeless man that I saw passing the window each day. I was so scared of him. He may have been an angel keeping his eye on me. He always seemed to be looking at me. Even when he passed the apartment he looked in my direction. I walked up and down the street crying. One time I was crying so hard and I stopped and had a seat on the comer of one of the businesses. A police drove by and looked at me. He told me that I had to move. He asked me what was wrong and he asked me was I drunk. I guessed I looked like a runaway to him. So I told him I was o.k. and that I was just upset. He told me that I couldn't sit on the property and asked me to move.

I headed towards the apartment and I heard something that sounded like thunder. Boom, Boom Boom, Boom Boom! It was Wayne's speakers. I could hear him before I saw him. He was blasting Houdini on his tape player. I walked a little faster as I missed him and I felt a little relief. When I got to the corner, he was turning in and he slowed down. He took one look at me and asked "what's wrong with you"? I asked him where he had been and this time he didn't offer any excuse. He asked me why I was walking around looking stupid. Then he went and parked his car. I told him that I was leaving. He chased me into the house. I ran into the bathroom and locked the door. He was right behind me. He knocked the door right off the hinges and tore into me like he was crazy.

We tore up Debbie and Donnell's bathroom. I was balled up in the floor when Debbie came into the bathroom and from the look on her face I knew I was a mess. Wayne left out and he, Donnell and Donnell's guest were watching t.v. I was so embarrassed, but I came out of the bathroom, and, Debbie and I talked.

Later that night, Wayne and I were in bed and I was in a whole lot of pain. I couldn't stand straight up. He joked. "What's wrong with your eye"? And me being dumb I laughed with him. After we had sex I was in so much pain and I begged him to please take me to the hospital. He took me to the Naval Hospital and I wore my glasses. I understood that I was not to tell anyone what happened even though Wayne and I had not discussed the secret. I was learning what to say and what not to say, especially after the time he beat me for telling someone that we did not have a child. He hit me like I was a man.

So there I was lying there on the table with my sunshades on and the doctor came over to me. He noticed the tears streaming down my cheek and into my ear. He asked me "Mrs. Burke, did he hit you"? I couldn't talk, I just cried. He told me that I had been hit in the kidney really hard and that I was just sore. He seemed to be more concerned with my obvious abuse. He asked again "why did he hit you Mrs. Burke"? He told me to get dressed and when he came back he led me into a small office. There sat a Navy-man with all of the colors on his shoulder. He was obviously a ranking superior. He asked me the same thing as my husband got escorted into the office. He asked my husband "Are you beating your wife"? I never said a word.

Wayne looked at the officer and told him "Yeah, I hit her; she know why I hit her." I felt like nothing.

I felt like the officers were thinking that I had done something to deserve this brutal attack. Wayne, having no respect for the Navy men, had his chest stuck out like he was proud of what he did. He was quite satisfied, as it seemed that he was going to get away with this one more time. I felt like I shouldn't tell because no one could help me. We returned to Debbie and Donnell's house and remained there for a couple of weeks. Christmas was approaching and so was our anniversary.

One morning we woke up and Debbie asked Wayne would he give her some money for Christmas dinner. He cursed her out. She told him that he was only supposed to stay for a couple of days and that we had gotten real comfortable. She looked at me and asked "What did he ever give you besides that baby?" I just stood there, floored because in reality, he hadn't done anything for me, nor given me anything not even a baby. I was so embarrassed.

Debbie knew that he was beating me and she had lost respect for both me and him. I guess she wondered why I stayed with him. She asked us to leave. Wayne and I were homeless again and we slept on the beach. I woke up that Christmas on the beach. It was about 100 degrees and the sun was shining. I remembered home. I wished that I were home. There were no presents, no Christmas dinner and even if I wanted to pretend that there was a Santa; there was no chance with not even a strong wind for him to ride in on. I wanted to die.

One day we looked in the paper and found an Apartment in Vista. We went to the office and the lady told us that she had a vacancy. She explained that it would be ready in one week. I began to cry. She asked, "Where are you sleeping at honey?" I told her that we were sleeping in the car and she told us that the place was just painted, but we could have it if we wanted.

She gave us the key and we moved in that day. Wayne made arrangements to pay her later. I thought that we would make it this time. This was a nice one-bedroom and in a nice complex. It looked so luxurious when you looked outside because at the center of the complex there were these beautiful flowers.

We had collected our things from Antwan's house and I was surprised that Janet was glad to see me. We moved into the place with the same little stuff that we had in Oceanside. Wayne announced later that week that in a few months that he was going overseas. He did not want me to stay in California. He wanted me to go back home. I had no choice, but for the time being I enjoyed our apartment. Everyday I got up to walk to the near-by shopping center. I would go inside the Big Bear daily and steal dinner for the night.

One day Wayne came in and he was upset. He told me that he was in trouble because of the report the Navy hospital gave the commander. He told me that we had to go to counseling. He looked at me as if it were all my fault saying, "We don't need counseling, do we?" I was so afraid to get him upset, so I agreed with him. I didn't know that in addition to the report that the Naval Hospital had, my grandmother hunted and searched until she found his chaplain's information. She had sent him a letter, so everyone was fully aware of the situation and the one time that I could have a chance to get help, I let him talk me out of it that quick.

I felt a little more at ease knowing that the next time my husband hit me that there would be some real consequences. One night right after my husband's 21st birthday, he announced that he was going to a real club and not the *"Enlisted Club"* that we had been going out to. I didn't understand why I couldn't go and why would he go out without me. We were doing so well. I protested and I tried to dress as fast as I could. The only thing that I had to wear was a wool, pleated suit. My hair was done and I went outside to wait on him. He crawled into his car on the passenger's side and locked the doors behind him. I sat up on the spoiler, sure that he wouldn't pull off with me sitting on top of the car. Boy, was I wrong. He pulled off and drove off the parking lot and into traffic as fast as he could. I was holding on to the spoiler for my life. There were cars riding behind us and they saw everything I had because my dress flew all the way up. I couldn't pull it down, because if I had let go, I wouldn't be telling this story.

My husband would be leaving for Japan soon and we were going back east before he left. The weekend before we left, Janet and Antwan came over to the house. I was glad to see them and their children. We looked at t.v. and I cooked for them. I really enjoyed Janet. Later Antwan and Wayne left and went to Janet's house to get high. They juggled us around so that they could get high. When

Janet told Antwan that he wasn't going to leave her again, they started to smoke cocaine right there in our faces. I had no idea what this stuff was, but it was clear that every night he had been gone that this was the other woman. He looked at her with so much desire. He placed those lips that I loved to kiss on her stem and he pulled her in so intimately. The look on his face as he removed the stem from his drooling lips was the look he used to have right after some good sex. I knew I could never compete with that. I didn't care. We were going home the next day. Finally, we would be going home together, the way we left.

Although there were signs before marriage, I did not take heed. I was so focused on running from the torch and jumped right into the fire. But, of course these things were not visible to me at that time. I felt that if I loved him enough he would change for me. But how could I love him when I didn't even love me; didn't even know me. It is so painful to look at my marriage after thirteen years of separation. I really thought that I had gotten better with the whole thing. I told myself that I forgave him. But Jesus made me take another look and this time.... I saw myself. I had nothing to do all day but consume soap operas. Every time one of the characters had an affair, my husband did too. My life became parallel to the soap stars, only mine was real life.

Of all the horror that I went through in this marriage, Yes, I'm finally seeing how broken I was and it is very painful. It's so easy to blame others and so hard to look at ourselves, but the truth of it is that you attract to yourself people who have something in common with you. In our case, a broken person attracted another broken person and Jesus wasn't anywhere in the midst. So while looking back what I found was myself, always judging him and always on his back. The truth is that he was doing the best he could with what he was working with. Then came the drugs. We both smoked marijuana and sometimes we drank. Once we tried Crystal Meth and I hated it. I was never so depressed in my life. He progressed to smoking cocaine. He tried everything to keep that from me. He would stay out nights and days. When he got home I would be so mad and we would fight. I really looked down on him when I found out what he was doing. We were moving from place to place, living with other couples and every time we got put out I was so humiliated. I was so down and I wished for death. I remember just asking God to take me on home. I put that man down so much, that being bone of his bone and flesh of his flesh, I was ordered to walk in his shoes for seven years.

Chapter Six

THE SEPARATION

While my husband was overseas, I met a man. He treated me like I thought a woman should be treated and we became intimate. I had gotten pregnant by this man and felt that I had to have an abortion. I don't know what hurt me more; the fact that I was becoming everything that I accused my husband of or that I had killed my first child as badly as I wanted a baby. I was in so much guilt.

I was sure to never cheat on him again, until, I met Sarita. This girl pulled me up in the dressing room of a store that she worked in. I was with a friend from high school who was obviously gay, but I never accepted it until then. She had her girlfriend with her. I was telling them about my adventures in California and she told me that I shouldn't have married him. We were in the store trying on clothes when Tria came to the dressing room. "Someone wants to meet you," I remember getting so nervous. I protested. "I don't want to meet no woman."

When I came out of the dressing room, there she was. She was beautiful. Fair-skinned with beautiful curly black hair. I felt my legs shaking as she introduced herself. "Hi, my name is Sarita. I looked into her eyes and said "Hi my name is Sarita." I felt myself about to break a sweat and I was embarrassed that this female made me forget my name. She talked me into going out to the club with them that night. When I got there I loved it. The music was a little different than what I was used to. After the club was closed, this girl that I danced with offered to take us home. She told Sarita that she was going to take me home last. Sarita got mad at her. When Sarita got out of the car, she turned to me and kissed me, sticking her long tongue all up in my mouth. This caused me to throw up. After that night, I couldn 't get her off my mind. There she was in full affect that lesbian demoness that had been preparing me for this moment my whole life. This wouldn't be considered cheating, this wasn't another man. We were getting pretty tight, never moving without each other. I was working at The Hecht Company doing hair and was doing all right for myself. I told Sarita that it was over, that my husband was on his way home.

When my husband came home from Japan I tried even harder to make this marriage work. The beatings had stopped and I guessed that it was because we were closer to our families. The cheating didn't stop though. That just got worse. I found phone numbers from women all the way from Japan. It was apparent to me that this marriage was over. I was working and he would run the street all day. We were living with my grandparents.

One day, my husband told me that he was going to do something real crazy. And he did! He stayed out for three days, I was so hurt and a little worried, but that's when I made up my mind that this is it. I was in my grandfather's basement crying and he told me to shut up. He told me "never mind, go ahead and cry now, because with that dude you will be crying for the rest of your life." I continued to see my husband from time to time and sometimes I would drop him off at his girlfriend's house. I was a complete fool for him. I was tired of being that fool. I worked two jobs to keep my mind off of him.

Meanwhile, I was dating a woman who picked me up in a clothing store. I really enjoyed the intimacy of the relationship. I found out later that she was the only woman that I had ever gotten close to besides my mother and she would protect me. I was trying everything to fill the void that I felt in my life since childhood. One night while I was working my second job, a Jamaican man came into the store and he asked me" What do you smoke besides cigarettes?" I paused and then I told him that I smoke pot. He asked, "What do you smoke besides pot and cigarettes?" I didn't remember that you could smoke anything else Cocaine didn't come to mind. This man gave me some crack and he left. It was crushed and I thought that it was cocaine. I tried snorting it and rocks were falling from my nose. I thought to myself what kind of man was this to come in my store and give me something that I did not ask for and it wasn't real. The man came back and I thought, "He sure got a nerve." I went out to his car and I told him that the cocaine wasn't real and he told me that I wasn't doing it right. While he was holding a cigarette he took a lighter and ran the flame up and down the cigarette. When the cigarette was wet he started smoking it. When he passed it to me I had found my new love.

At first the lifestyle seemed so glamorous. I was working two jobs and drug trafficking. The money was plenty and I didn't have to buy any drugs. It wasn't very long before I'd quit both my jobs and straight to the bottom I went. I was stealing and selling my body for it within a year. I tried geographical cures. I moved to California with my lesbian friend to get away from the drugs that had taken over my life. She and I ended up getting high together. I came back home.

I went back and forth a few times and finally I was home to stay. I met another woman and it seemed that all we did was get high. I remember one day on the bus and our discussion became public. I remember her telling me that we weren't getting high the right way. I told her that no matter how I do it I always feel the same afterwards. I told her that by the time I was thirty I wanted to have a family and not be getting high anymore. I was only 23.

Chapter Seven

GOING IN DEEPER

The next 6 years of my life would was hell. I believe the Lord heard my pledge because he snatched me right out of the jaws of the devil at 29.

I had a guy front me in a Beauty business. This was my salon. It's funny how life would trick me over and over again into thinking that things were getting better. I met a man and fell in love. I think because he sold cocaine. I started stealing from him and he had so much cocaine that he didn't even notice or he never did say. I told him one day that I was getting high and if he wanted his cocaine to take it with him.

I went into a seven day detox. I left before seven days. I found out that I was pregnant and things were over between he and I. While I was pregnant, I saw my girlfriend and she told me that she had gotten me pregnant. I haven't been with a woman since that day.

I felt that if this lifestyle would lead me into this kind of denial, thinking that I was a man, then I had better leave this thing alone.

Here I was pregnant again, broken hearted and I was still smoking crack. I went into a treatment center in my seventh month. Once baby got here I was still getting high. I still loved her father. Once we tried to live together, and as much as I wanted to do right, I had no control. After that relationship was over I started tricking to support my habit. It got so that I would do anything for another hit. Anything! I didn't care who saw me anymore. I would stand out on the corner and sell my body for drugs. I sold the coat off my back in a snowstorm. I was trapped in a world that I couldn't get out of.

I went into a treatment center every year it seems only to start over again. My daughter knew very little of me. I hated myself for that. Every time I would stop getting high, all of the things I did came to mind and shame ran me back to the drugs. At this point my choice was to die out there or to face all of the pain of my past. I would always choose death. I would find myself on Sunday morning standing in front of a church looking for a trick. And it seemed like I would always see a funeral drive by and I would see my family in the cars. I just knew that this was my funeral. I don't know if that was a vision or not. I questioned the idea of funerals being held on Sunday.

I think God was trying to tell me something. Things just got worse. On one of my clean up sprees, I went to visit a friend in recovery. I slept with him and there came baby number two. When I told him that I was pregnant, he hung up the phone on me. When I told my family, they turned their back and I couldn't blame them.

Here I was pregnant again and wasn't taking care of my first child. Everyone, including my mother told me to get an abortion and this time I couldn't. I just couldn't.

I met another drug dealer and mentioned to him that I was pregnant and was going to be put in the street. We became friends. I went into another treatment center and when I got out I went to live in his rental property. He fixed it up really nice for me, bought me maternity clothes and the money that I gave him for rent he would spend it back on me.

There were two problems; he sold drugs and he was married. I started using drugs again during my pregnancy and was getting high when I went into labor. He stood by my side anyway until he went to prison. Another one of life's tricks, I thought I had something. I didn't mind falling from the curb to the gutter, but it was a hard fall from what I considered to be the top. The wife and the son put me out. My grandparents came and picked up my oldest daughter, my mother came to get the baby and the dog. No one came to get me and I attempted suicide. My grandfather finally showed up and I ended up in another treatment center. This time I really tried to stay clean. I started going to school to study computers and I spent the rest of my time with the girls.

Chapter Eight

THE BIG RELAPSE

One Christmas Eve, the first Christmas that I had ever done anything for my children, I put everything under the tree and then a craving came up on me so heavy. I could not fight it. There were still issues that I wasn't dealing with. For one thing my daughter's father was getting married and he did not show up with her toys when I wanted him to. The truth was that I still loved him and I was getting myself together for him. I always felt that we could get back together, but God knew best. I was busy trying to sue my friend's wife for my furniture that they took from me. Here I was the victim again and I never once considered that God had brought me out. It was impossible to stay clean without God. So I went out that Christmas Eve and I got high.

Of course I couldn't stop after that first night. This run would continue for seven months. These seven months would complete my seven years of using drugs. This was also the worst run that I had. I was sitting in this apartment and there was a little girl there. Her crack smoking guardian was Muslim so he couldn't feel the way I did about Christmas. This little girl was the one who reminded me of my kids, so I left there crying.

I thought that I would die. Christmas morning, I wasn't there for my children and that broke my heart. I wanted so much to be dreaming, but it was real. It took me one night to get right back to where I was ten months ago. And I even wished for a miracle like death so I wouldn't have to face my family and my kids and try to explain what I couldn't. When daylight came, I began to cry.

There was a guy in the crack house. I feared this guy. Everybody knows that he has killed before. He asked me why I was crying. I told him that this was the first Christmas that I had brought my kids some toys and I wasn't there to see them open their stuff. He tried to comfort me by saying that he had never brought his kids anything. That was precisely my point. Until this Christmas, I was never able to do anything for my kids. But this time... This time I had finally got a glimpse of who I was and I had even learned to like me a little. I was beginning to experience the joy of being a mother. If you never knew joy, you would not miss it. But I had been given a chance to be a mother again, I had been back with my family and they trusted me again.

Everything that I had worked so hard for was gone including school and the relationship with my family. I met a man that invited me to his house. He let both me and my crack into his home. One time I was in his bathroom smoking and when I came out, I found him praying for me. I didn't know then, but later he told me that he prayed that no one would want to be near me. They wouldn't want me in their home or in their midst. He must have prayed for my protection also because this time I know that God carried me through. I escaped death and prison many, many times.

I started to wonder why God would not let me die, I had become comfortable with the fact that I was going straight to hell and the sad part was that I didn't care. I met another guy named Paul. He was an older guy and he smoked crack. After being chased away from all of the other crack houses, this guy would let me come in, and, he and I would smoke. What was the turning point? Well one day Paul and I was smoking. We smoked up all of the money that we had. This was the one day that proved to me that a thousand was never enough. We had gotten high all day, all night and the next morning. While he was asleep I stole his car. I was driving around hacking for one hit at a time. I met a girl who had another hustle and that was the fast food restaurants. She would call them and complain about food she never brought and they would give her money. Once she got the money from the second restaurant, we went into her neighborhood to buy the crack.

The guy that took our money walked across the street and he saw another guy. I don't know what this guy did to him, but he started to beat him half to death. Then the neighborhood joined in. I know it was ten guys or better beating the hell out of this guy. He was riding a bike and they beat him with that bike. Something in my soul stirred, but my mind was on my next hit. Someone shot the guy and just like any gunshot, people started to run. The guy was able to get up and make it over to the car that I had stolen and got in. He told me with his mouth dripping blood "Please pull off". I told the guy to get out of the car. He held on to the armrest. "Please help me." Just then the guys came and pulled him from the car. He tore out the armrest and took it with him. That's how tight he was holding on. Me, all I could think about was my next hit. I was becoming a monster and I was just as bad as the guys who beat him and probably even killed him. That wasn't my concern. I just wanted to get high.

So, I finally got out of there without my next hit and I continued to hack. I would have to get another hit before I take Paul his car back. I would have to get another hit to help me forget what I had just witnessed. I made a few more stops until I ran into this guy who was all of fourteen. He didn't want a ride anywhere he wanted to trick. I slept with this kid for two vials of crack. He told me to drop him off somewhere. He had a dog with him. So I started to drive. I stopped at the 7-11 to get a pack of cigarettes and he stayed in the car. When I got out of the store, Paul's car was gone. The shock of this whole thing immediately made my cycle begin.

I still managed to catch a ride, another trick. They took me halfway back uptown. Then another guy would pick me up on his way to church. I never told this guy that I was on my period and he tricked with me, in broad daylight, up in the alley. I made a mess all over this man's car and all over him. The man started to cry. He told me that he was married. I left his car and another guy from that neighborhood took me in and washed my clothes and tricked with me. I left there and got high once more before going back to Paul's. When I got back, Paul was angry, but he allowed me in his house. He told me that the police had been there and that he reported the car stolen. He told me that the kid had totaled his car. I didn't know if the kid died or if he was injured; I didn't know if the man who was beaten died or not; and I didn't know if I had wrecked this man's marriage or not. Once I was sober enough to realize all of this, I cried so hard. I knew I wanted to make a change, but I didn't know how I would. How could I? I had gone too far.

One day I had gone back to Tony's house. He was the guy that I met on Christmas Eve. He left me in his house one morning while he went to cop. I was smoking and something told me to put the pipe down. Something burned through my back and I felt someone was looking at me. I put down the pipe and turned around and I noticed the same little girl. She was just sitting in her bed looking at me. I went into her room and I asked her if she was o.k. She said that she was hungry. This broke my heart. She was sitting in a soiled bed. She would not even get up to go the bathroom. I don't think that she was allowed. I remembered the many times that I went there and she was always in the bed. I started looking for her clothes. She had a few pieces and they were all small. I looked for her toys and there was none. I asked myself, "what about Christmas." Then I remembered that I was there Christmas morning and there was no Christmas at her house. The grinch had stolen Christmas from two homes that year.

I went into the kitchen to get her something to eat and the cupboard was bare. Tony was taking so long. I threw on the pieces that she had to wear and I took her to my grandmother's. They looked at me like I was crazy. Here I come with another kid and I wasn't taking care of my own. Then I was able to feed this little girl. I noticed that her coordination was off and that she couldn't even maneuver the fork straight into her mouth. God revealed to me then that this was a crack baby and that it was only by his grace that my kids were not developmentally delayed just like she was. I kept her with us all day long and when I was about to take her back, she screamed "Please don't take me back" I was torn apart. I had to take her back but I told myself that if I ever got clean that I would remember her. One of the promises God allowed me to keep.

I would stay out for four days straight and then go home in no shape to care for my kids. I would rest up for a day and get right on about the business of killing myself. I found myself in so many terrible situations. Life threatening situations. I remember the time when I was prostituting, or tricking if you will. Sometimes I got twenty dollars, sometimes I got ten dollars, sometimes I got drugs, sometimes I got dry wall and sometimes I got nothing. Getting nothing for my sexual favors was not the worst thing that could happen though. Sometimes I would get beaten.

I remember performing with two guys, only to have them throw me from a moving car when I was done. This was hell. Getting high became a chore. I remember that I spent more time on the street trying to get money for drugs (getting low) than I actually spent getting high. I was raped on several occasions and I couldn't tell anyone. Who would listen to a crack head? I slept with anybody to get drugs. Once I was clean, God revealed the people that I had slept with that actually had the HIV virus and some had died from AIDS. I slept with AIDS unprotected and I was all right with the fact that I would die with this or either a drug overdose. I had given up as I found myself, once again, on the comer in front of this church one Sunday morning, witnessing my funeral ride by.

Chapter Nine

ANOTHER CHANCE

God was so forgiving. He gave me another chance.
One day I was standing in front of a church and two
men walked out of the church and up the street towards
me and I asked them did they know Jesus. See I had tried
everything else but Jesus. The gentlemen told me that they
new the man, I asked them to pray for me. Surely God
would not listen to me; I let Him down so much. But He
heard my cry. He saw this filthy rag and picked me up and
held on to me as if I were a precious thing. And to God,
I was precious.

Imagine now! Everyone had taken their hands off
of me. So it wasn't hard to grasp the fact, once I was
clean this time, that it was God that had performed this
miracle in my life. Everyone wanted to know, what will
be different this time? I couldn't answer this question. I
remember being so disturbed about this, but the fact of
the matter was I didn't even know how I was maintaining
that moment and I didn't know what would be different.
This was God's business and I know that answer now. But
only through the grace of God. He revealed this answer to
me a day at a time. Still then I only had an idea of God.
My belief in God went only to the extent that somebody

saved my life and it wasn't people. That was a start. That was all that God needed to perform his mighty plan for my life. Just a little faith. Just an acknowledgement of Him made the difference in my living or dying.

They say if you don't remember your last hit, then it probably wasn't your last. Well I remember going to get drugs from some girls that I feared. It was obvious that they didn't like me, but there was nowhere else to go. I sat there with one of the girls and she was nice to me. She told the other girls that no matter how high we were I would never steal from her. We all found this out the hard way. One day she and her girls thought that I had taken some drugs from her and they came after me. I wrote a poem about this. The day God came into the crack house to get me.

"GOD DON'T BLESS NO MESS"

This statement had been globalized
It's in pulpits across the nation
I heard it proclaimed on TBN
And on my gospel radio station

This one statement got recognition
And it pierced our hearts with repetition
It left me empty and fervently wishing
That even my dreams would come to fruition

So one day I searched the Bible
For this profound revelation
I was sure to find it there
If only I were patient

I searched as I hungered
For this life changing word
I tired so I stopped to rest
On Matthews 23rd

Woe to the Pharisees
Is what I surely heard
"You shut the kingdom of heaven
In the faces of men."
Probably because you yourself
Have not entered in

You say you come in the name of our Lord
And you stand there and proclaim

That God Won't Bless No Mess
Come on here Saints, let us confess:

When the Lord God found us
We were stained
With sin and sickness
Sadness and pain
Pride and Envy
Jealousy and Greed

And God required us to believe
Having faith as small as a mustard seed
God gave so much and required so little
Now the dying are outside trying to get in
And the Saints are in the middle

People are watching you
And they hear you when you say
"That God will never bless a mess;
There is just no way"

We're suppose to edify
To speak life to the dying
To show love to the suffering
To come forth testifying

That while we were yet sinners
Christ Jesus died to save us
And all the things that we had done
The faithfully forgave us

And even though we're saved
We're still wrapped in flesh
And as much as we try to please the Lord
Our lives are still a mess.

God has never blessed a situation
But his children he will bless
He'll use what Satan meant to kill you
To make your tongues confess.

One day before I knew the King
I was into everything

I was married and then I separated
I hived with a married man

I had one chihd and one on the way
Standing on sinking sand

Addicted to drugs and thirty days clean
But still my life was so obscene
One day I'd found my boyfriend's stash

I was back where I started in a flash
Back in the crack house on Allendale
My attempt to get clean
Was to no avail

I sat in this CRACK HOUSE smoking crack
I heard someone upstairs being attacked
I got really nervous I've been here before
Soon the Police would be at the door

Raye

I gathered my things
Before the police could come
I didn't want to go to jail
Pregnant and looking dumb

I walked out of the back door
Down through the alley

I crossed the main highway
That cut right through the valley

I made it half way down the street
When four women grabbed me
I was dragging my feet
I thought that they might stab me

What did they want?
What did I do?
They said that I had stolen their drugs
Of course it wasn't true

They dragged me back,
Across the street
Through the alley and in the back,
They poured out everything I had
Looking for their crack.

One of the girls shouted
"I think found my stuff
My anxiety was on overhead
I thought I'd had enough

Just then the Police came
bursting through the door
They immediately explained
What they were there for

Someone called us
and told us that they saw
A pregnant woman was being dragged
And so here we are

They looked at me with compassion
And said "Are you alright"
I thought I was just because
I wouldn't sit in jail all night

It took me many years to see this
I was so confused
And if anyone called the police
I don't hnow who God used

But I know that I was a mess then
And not far from it now
But the Lord still loves me anyway
And blesses me somehow.

I went into my last drug treatment center and I was oblivious. I got high right up until 2:00 am and I was to go into the treatment center at 8:00. It was later revealed that this last run lasted for seven months. I was crack addicted for seven years. My last run was seven months to the hour. God said, "It is finished."

After treatment, I went to meetings and also an individual session with Ms. Harriet Brown. She was a dynamic woman and a voice that I would hear far beyond the nine months of meeting with her. I was able to go back to school and finish studying information processing. I was able to become a mother to my kids again. I was able to form a relationship with my mother again, on her terms. I was pleased with every moment that I was able to share with her. She was truly the apple of my eye.

During the first months of recovery, my stepfather and my sister were doing their thing and this left time for me. Even when my sister was around, my mother would ask me to drive them to the mall. I had no money and two kids and sometimes I would feel hurt because I would have to sit in the eatery and wait on my mom and sister, while they shop. She would give me five dollars and we'd split a slice of pizza and a soda. My mother acted as though I wasn't her daughter. I was the lowly chauffer or something. I remember being on social services and when my food stamps would come she would take me shopping for food. She would ask me to get her some food. I distinctly remember feeling that I shouldn't do for her because she didn't do anything for me, but God would immediately step in and I would be more than glad to help her.

It was then that God revealed that my mom was being abused. I had enough experience with abuse to recognize this and I had a little information to deal with the fact that I could not save her any more than she could save me. We became friends. I would go to meetings and therapy and call her every day. I was anxious to share information with her. It was revealed to me that expecting my mother to be a mother to me again was of less importance. She didn't have what it took. She was already spread too thin. I wanted to nurture her. I wanted to take care of her. I started witnessing the abuse from my sister and the neglect from my stepfather. The two people that I felt had taken her away didn't appreciate her like I did. Damn, that hurt me. I remember being in the car with her one day and she was telling me that she felt like God was punishing her for what she let happen to me. She looked at me and she asked "You and I have a pretty good relationship now, don't we?" Surprised at the notion, I shook my head "Yes." I knew that I wanted more from my mother, but I was so pleased to accept the little that she gave of herself. We were becoming closer than ever. I loved every moment of this. I appreciated every little thing that she gave.

I remember our last Christmas together. I went over to her house and she was cooking her dinner. She was the best cook in the world. She wanted to put up the Christmas tree and I helped her. It was just the two of us like many, many years before and I was so happy. We played carols and put up the tree and it was more special to me than anything. God gave me in a short period of time, memories that would last me for the rest of my life. I am so grateful to Him for this, even today. That Christmas I was able to spend with my mother, my kids and I was able to share Christmas with the little girl that I had met.

Chapter Ten

ANOTHER VISION

It was March 19th 1996. That night I went to bed and dreamed that I was inside a mall and that I saw an old friend. Lucy. She was our neighbor for years and she was an alcoholic. Her daughter was one of my childhood friends. I saw her in the mall and she looked so good. Having a recovery consciousness, I immediately asked her "How long have you been clean?" She answered and told me that she was clean for three years. I was so glad to see her and I wanted more than anything to share this with my mother. So, I began looking for my mother throughout the mall. I went to Nordstrom and Macy's and Lord and Taylor's. Stores I wouldn't dare enter for any other reason than to find my mother. This was so normal because they continuously shopped in these stores and after I had gotten tired of waiting for them in the eatery, I would begin my search. Finally I had found my mother and I was telling her to come with me because I wanted her to see Lucy. When we got back to Lucy, she was crying so hard. I asked her why was she crying and she told me that they wouldn't let her hold the baby. I asked her what baby and she moved to the side. On this bed was a little infant boy.

Knowing a little about dreams, having had them all of my life, I knew that an infant at least sometimes represented death. I woke up that morning and I began to process this dream. The only thing that wasn't revealed to me was who was going to die. I remember that Lucy's family had gone through death after death and there were hardly any of them left. So I thought that it was my friend Lamika. I woke up that morning and called my mother. She was not home. Within the hour she was calling me. "Tammy, ask Sis what size do Russell wear?" She was shopping for my grandfather's birthday. I told her that I had this dream about Lucy. She didn't act as though that was important at that time. I asked her could she take me to school and she grumbled and mumbled but finally she said yes.

When she arrived over at my grandmother's house, where I was staying, she asked me what it was that I was trying to tell her on the phone. "You dreamed about a net," she asked. "No, I replied. "I dreamed about Lucy and she was so beautiful. She was clean for three years. Ma, she's been dead about three years." I told her about the baby and then I asked her was there anyway that we could find Lamika. She said she didn't know. I felt desperate to talk to Lamika and to warn her. I hadn't talked to Lamika since the time that I was kidnapped and raped five years earlier.

My mother was so unconcerned with what I was telling her. She took me to school and dropped me off. After school, I went to dinner with a friend and while sitting there eating, I got a page from my mother. This was so peculiar, she never paged me. I called her and let her know that I was all right. She said that she just wanted to make sure. I very rarely made a move without letting her know where I would be. We spoke briefly and I called her back once I was at home. That night she sounded so good and so peaceful. The next morning she was gone. It never dawned on me that the one that I spent most of that dream trying to find was also the one that I would lose.

The phone rang that morning and I was in the bed. The phone was in my grandmother's room and I could hear my sister screaming through the phone. My grandmother replied, "No, she's not dead." I fell out of the bed backwards and started looking for clothes and shoes. "Just get me to her God and I know that she will be all right. This was another one of those calls where my sister just went a little too far Mom may have been sick, but if God would just get me there she would be all right." A drive that usually took about fifteen minutes seemed like it was taking forever. I rocked back and forth in the car and prayed. "God, please let my mother be alright."

When we approached her street, there were lights every where. The whole street was lit up with emergency vehicles. We could hardly get to the door. I went up on the porch and my sister ran to us, crying. "Tammy, you have to see her." I tried to get into the house and the paramedics would not let me in. So I sat on the porch and waited. They came to the door a few times and asked us was she taking any drugs. They continued to work on her.

Finally, they told me to go next door. I stood in the neighbor's door and watched them roll her body out. I watched that gurney as it rolled out of the driveway. Her head was uncovered and I had hope. Then I saw that her body jiggled as they went over the bumps in the road.

Then I saw her feet and they were blue. I knew at this point that she was dead. My prayer changed from that moment from "God, please let her live" to "God please help me." We followed the ambulance to the hospital and within minutes, the nurses came out and said that she had passed.

This was the most difficult time in my life and I just knew that I would get high over this. This was the one time that I had a good enough reason to use and I would take advantage of this, in spite of the fact that I had chaired two meetings that week and in both meetings I told other addicts that even if your mom dies, you never have to use again. Little did I know that those words that I had spoken to these two groups of people would be the words that would save my life. I am grateful to God for keeping me even when I didn't know that I could be kept. Even when I didn't want to be kept. I grieved so hard. I was so pitiful as the family lined up behind me to go inside the sanctuary. I walked in and took a look at my mother in that casket. I went into a complete fit. All of my denial had left me and the fact that I never went to view the body didn't help. I was supposed to sit on the first row but I went past that row and sat on the second row on the end with my back turned to the coffin. When I saw my mother in that box, a part of me died with her. I never knew pain like this and I had to do it all sober.

Chapter Eleven

"YE OF LITTLE FAITH"

I was about 90 days clean from drugs and alcohol as I lay in the bed one Sunday morning and the Lord spoke to me and told me to go to church. I called my mother and told her that I wanted us to go to church together. So she came over to pick me up and we went to church. While sitting there I felt like a sore thumb. I never really fit into the church, especially since I had turned my whole life over to Satan. This was the first church that I stepped into since God had delivered me and I was feeling awkward. I had on a red sleeveless mini-skirt set with black polka dots, no stockings and black heel shoes. My bony, hairy legs looked like wooden sticks. I felt so uncomfortable. So there we sat. I don't remember the message, but what I do remember is that day my mother and me both gave our life back to the Lord. We were standing down front with the pastor who married both my mother and I. We were holding hands. I feel that is the greatest memory that I have of my mother. She was abused as a child, abandoned and she could only give me what she had. So it appeared that we were close, and at some point we were, but she wasn't the hugging kissing mom that I always told myself she was. I had high expectations of her, and I lived the fantasy through television, through boys, through drugs. It took me years to find out that she wasn't really connected to me emotionally. So the day we stood before God holding hands and rededicating our lives to Him was the most beautiful thing. To be honest, I didn't see God. All I saw was my mom and I touching for the first time in years. Then here comes the pastor. He said that God had something for me to do. I asked my mom on the way home "What do you think it is that God wants me to do. Take this mini skirt off?" She laughed.

Well, we continued to go to church every Sunday for a little while until she and my sister had taken up shopping on Sunday. I was hurt. I was angry. I felt that from the time I was seven someone was taking my mom from me and for a moment I had her hand and now it has slipped away, again.

I continued on my road to recovery and I remained in the fellowship of Narcotics Anonymous, but I had nothing to do with church. Even though, while I was there I did hear some things. My mom passed away shortly thereafter. Here I stand at the crossroads. Not knowing where to turn. The single most important person in my life was gone. I was faced with something that I never had much of and that is a choice. I was cleaned up enough to make a decision that would affect the rest of my life.

Well, of course at that point I did nothing. I stayed at the crossroads for a long time. I was devastated without my mother, but what I noticed is that the major resentments in my life were centered on my mother. I resented my stepfather because he took her from me. I was angry with my sister because she had my mom's full attention. I was angry with my mom because she didn't protect me from my stepfather's abuse and she did not let my sister know that I was also her child. All of these things I carried and all of these things I used drugs over.

About three months after the death of my mother, I went on a Christian Woman's Retreat. I thought this would be great. I would get a chance to get away and plus it was free. I really enjoyed the ride up there. The person that I sat next to on the bus, the conversation, and the games that we played were more than enough to keep my mind off of my dilemma. Wow, I was laughing again for the first time in months. It felt great! I was spending a lot of time focusing on God and Jesus. Only because this is what was going on around me. I was in a lost state. I was in between living and dying. I was in between Islam and Christianity. I was still at the crossroads of my life. At the crossroads. Let's talk about the crossroads for a moment. This is where I started. I was at a crossroads when I decided to smoke cigarettes. I was at the crossroads when I decided to begin having sex and doing drugs. I was at a crossroads when I decided to have my kids as oppose to aborting them. The crossroads to me is when you're at the point of a decision that will change your entire life and you have to choose.

When I was on drugs it appeared that I didn't have a choice in anything. So God had restored me to a level of sanity to where I could again make sound decisions. Not good or bad but sound.

I took a good look at my life on this trip and I was going to make a decision. That would be my goal for this weekend.

I stepped off of the bus onto Agape Farms and I was open-minded. Ready for the next step. I knew about God. There was no doubt in my mind. But I couldn't grasp this Jesus concept. The whole bit about some stranger dying for me, my sins being washed away. I was too guilty, but I was going to consciously try to grasp the concept.

The first day was laid back. We ate and we fellowshipped. There were powerful speakers. I was given a secret pal. She was giving me gifts the whole weekend. I was someone else's pal. I thought this was a great idea. They had books and tapes on sale. There was no television or music around. Nothing to focus on but God. I was going to enjoy this trip.

The next day after breakfast we were getting ready for the "Great Moun tain Walk." I heard the other woman talk about their mountain top experiences and I thought "Awesome." I mean these Christians were really on to something and I wanted to see this awesome power of God. We lined up and the minister was anointed our heads with oil. When it was my turn she said a few words and anointed my head. Afterwards, I waited for the group that I would be walking with. Another sister stepped up and she had about 90 days clean from drugs and alcohol. They prophesied to her and told her that she was being set free, but that wasn't it. It appeared to me that they were hitting her on the head. "In the name of Jesus," they shouted. They did this repeatedly until she passed out or fell down. This stuck in my head and I said to myself this is ridiculous. Why are they slapping on this poor lady? I remember that no one had to slap me to get free of drugs. But when this is over, I will ask her if she felt anything.

Did she experience this awesome power? And if she did, then why didn't I feel it too?

So we began to walk towards this huge mountain and finally we were starting to climb. Being a prisoner to more than a few things, I took out my pack of cigarettes and started to puff. I'm walking and puffing. Going to God just as I was and if he were God then he would accept me. This was my attitude. I continued to climb and smoke. I remember telling God that I don't have to see Jesus at the top of this mountain, but I'll settle for my mother. In any case I let it be known that I was expecting to hear from God. "Before I leave this mountain God I want to know if I am Christian or Muslim. Elijah or Jesus, God, that is all I want to know."

Finally we arrived. Everyone split up and did their own thing. Meditating, planting prayers in the mountain, praying and praising God. I went off and dug a hole and planted a prayer in the ground for my sponsor, who had sent me on the retreat in her place. Then I was lost. I felt alone. So I talked to God and I told God that I would not leave this mountain until he showed me something; until he gave me what I came there for. I looked around and I saw no spirits, no Jesus, not even my mother. I was disappointed. So I walked around waiting for the group to reassemble so that I could go back down and continue my stance at the crossroads. It was evident that my answer was not on this hill. Then I walked over to a boardwalk and I looked over. We were way up there. And the view was awesome. I noticed a little farm below and saw what appeared to be a bam. On top of the bam was the word "JESUS." That was my answer. No bright lights, no spiritual awakening, but God had given me my answer according to my little faith.

Just then my secret pal came over and prayed for me on that mountaintop and my life has been changed since that day. I figure if God can honor my little faith, he could move mountains with Great Faith. So I made a decision to follow Christ. Later my roommate and I were able to talk. I asked her about her experience. I wanted to know did she feel the spirit or did they just push her down. So I asked. She told me that she didn't know. She said, "I think I felt something." Then she asked "Do you think God was really telling her those things about me?" My reply: "God must have told her not to hit me because I would have hit her back," We laughed.

Chapter Twelve

SATAN IS A LIAR

A s soon as I professed Jesus to be my lord and savior, my life started to change gradually. I sat in church one night at prayer meeting after God had told me for the second time to go to this church. I thought that the last time he told me to go to church; it had to be for my mom. This time God was calling me. I went to prayer meeting because I felt that this was the only part of the service that I could use at the time. I remembered the words of the pastor when he told me that God had something for me to do. I was in church that night and the spirit moved me to testify. I didn't want to tell anyone in the church about my not so distant past, but I couldn't keep it to myself. I started sharing my story with others outside of the meetings and outside of therapy and people seemed to listen. I used my writing ability to create poetry. My mother had shared this among other things with a friend of hers. I talked to him and he invited me to an awards ceremony. He presented me an award for "Beating the Odds." I had never won anything in my life. I brought a beautiful gown and slid on some pumps and I felt fabulous. I wrote a poem and presented it that night. The name of the poem was "<u>Satan. You're a Liar.</u>" When they called my name, I stood up and I was shaking everywhere. I managed to read this poem aloud and this was the first time that I had ever presented my poetry. The words of this poem are my testimony.

SATAN, YOU 'RE A LIAR

Once upon a time they called me crackhead
My standards of living was that of an animal
Spiritually, mentally and emotionally dead
Lying, Cheating and stealing were my means of survival
The odds say that I would smoke crack until the day I die
Once an addict, always an addict, huh, Satan you're a lie
I always heard a voice inside of me, telling
me "Tammy you can be free.
You really don't have to live this way; Just
open your heart, repent and pray"

I started to talk back to this voice,
trying to make him understand
"Don't you see I had no choice, life
dealt me a messed up hand
You see I was abused all of my life, I was
someone's battered daughter
And someone's battered wife
I didn't know how to live and was too afraid to die
So you see, I just gave up, that is why I'm getting high"
A voice answered me and said "Tammy, you didn't try"

Then one day, I had gotten real sick,
Of people calling me names like crack head and trick

Sitting in guilt and shame so deep
Hurting so bad, I couldn't sleep
I thought about all of the things I did
To myself, my family and to my kids
Oh the Kids!

I thought about my pregnancies when I was getting high
Not being able to stop even though my kids might die
But, through God's grace and mercy,
My kids were born just fine
He did not let them suffer much, the suffering was mine

I thought about all the times that my life was spared
But I thought that no one loved me
and I felt that no one cared
Someone had to be there I was so powerless!!!!
So I opened my heart, repented, prayed
And behold my God's Goodness

People said that I would smoke crack until the day I die
Once a junky, always a junky, but Satan you're a lie
A day at a time the lord delivers me. I am drug free today
But I must keep my heart open, I must repent and pray

For anyone who will listen, I want
to share the goodness of God
You don't have to smoke crack to
know that life today is hard
There is nothing too great for God he'll always make a way
Remember to open your heart, repent
and don't forget to pray

When Satan makes life hard for you,
don't back down or be shy
Just turn around and say to him, "Satan, you're a lie"

I was so naive when it came to the things of God. I was about to learn my first lesson. I had publicly proclaimed Satan to be a liar and immediately he placed me under attack. Looking back I realized that I wanted to give God the glory and I did, but I wanted some glory too. I had invited a date to the ceremony and he stood me up. After standing there and reading my story aloud to non-addicts and some Christians, I was feeling good, but I didn't have the gratification that I thought I needed from a man so I acted out. I went to his house. I knew he was home. I rang the doorbell and his sister lied and told me that he was not there. This made me so angry. I drove to the back of his house where he had hid his car and damaged his vehicle. Now my career was complete. After several years of using drugs and coming out clean, now I had a criminal record for malicious destruction of property.

My walk with the Lord started out rough. I vowed never to read that poem aloud again. I didn't know that when I started praising God that it would offend Satan. I felt that if I didn't mess with Satan, then Satan wouldn't mess with me. I was so wrong. Everyday became a struggle for me because I wanted so much to do right and not rock the boat. I wanted peace among all things and I couldn't seem to find it anywhere. Then I realized that this was only the beginning and that I had a very long way to go. I was trying so hard to fit into this society that I had not been a part of for so long and still there was no place for me in it. I went to work, I came home to my children, I talked to other people and I tried to do everything that I saw so called normal people doing, but this wasn't it. I was still a very sick young woman. I still wanted to please people, and as hard as I thought it was to please God, this would prove to be ten times harder. I found out new things everyday about myself that I wanted to change, but I realized that I didn't have the power to change anything. I soon forgot that while I was yet a sinner Christ died for me. I still had a long road to travel before I would even surrender to this fact. I thought that God would love me because I was not doing drugs anymore. I thought that God would love me because I managed to go back to school and finish and get a job to take care of my kids. I thought that God would love me because I gave up prostitution. And, I was sure that he would love me for trying to please everyone. I missed the concept. God loved me while I was in the street smoking crack. I would have to accept this love in order to start loving myself and start forgiving myself.

One Sunday morning I was in the basement giving my God some praise the best way I knew how and God told me once more to go to church. I went back to that same church and I had made an appointment to talk with the pastor. I wanted to discuss what he told me. What did God have for me to do? He never showed up for the appointment and I was offended. I soon found out about people, even church people, especially church people. This kept me away from fellowship for a long time. Once I went back to that church to visit and I found out who the real pastor of that Church was. It was the lady from the old church. The one I grew up in. So when God told me to go back to that church that day to visit I was in for a surprise. The senior pastor had moved on and the female pastor was the speaker that day. She called me out of the congregation and told the church that I was going to evangelize some day. So as soon as I walked into that church, God had given me my answer.

This was good news and it was news that I wanted to share with everyone. This was not received by anyone that I loved and cared about. I was shocked. But I was in love with the fact that God wanted to use me. As messed up as I was and believe me everyone took this opportunity to remind me of the fact, people that I know who claim to love Jesus had such a problem with this. My perception of their behavior was that I was only allowed to go so far, as long as I did not exceed the level that they had placed themselves on. God was just beginning to reveal people to me and I had a lot to learn. Most of the people that I loved and cared about was pleased with the fact that I was clean and sober. This was as far as I was allowed to go. I could hear them saying under their breath, why would God use a crack head when he could use me. God revealed to me that he could use anyone that he chose. He probably chose a crack head because he knows that he and only he would get the glory out of someone as useless as I. Never the less I did as I always did. I backed out of the church completely. This would please my so-called loved ones. They could continue to go and come home and give me updates. This way they could take credit for me and my salvation. You know the devil is still a liar.

God had a plan that no one could destroy. God said that he would use me one day and I believe God. I started talking to God and then one day he started speaking to me. I always had visions, but now they were more clear and full of revelation. My writing became more of a ministry and I was seeing where God was building me up. Me, a broken vessel. I would share my visions that were revelation with my loved ones so that when a thing would come to pass they would know that God was indeed speaking to me. Even though I was not in the church. God was feeding me his word and giving me revelation and this was hard for people to understand. I could hear them saying "Why would God reveal that to you, when he has me."

Chapter Thirteen

THE PROPHETESS

One day I happened to call my aunt who we call Ehemiah, the prophetess. This phone call changed my life. I had not seen my father's sister in fifteen years and she spoke right into my life. I went to meet her shortly after that and I became obsessed with the fact that she could see things, she could hear from God and she confirmed the fact that God wanted to use me. I went to Virginia almost every two weeks to visit her and her friend Nicole. One day my aunt prayed for me and she snatched my glasses off and told me God said "Double vision." This was the first time that I had ever felt the Holy Spirit. The feeling was euphoric and it was the best thing I had ever felt since my first encounter with drugs. Naturally being who I am, I wanted that feeling again and again.

One night about two weeks later I was asleep and I had a vision. I was being lifted into outer space. I was so amazed at the stars all around me. It was breathtaking. I marveled at the creation and as I looked around me one star got brighter and brighter. I noticed it, but I would turn and look around again. There were so many stars I kept noticing new ones, but this one star got closer and finally it took the shape of an angel. This angel reached out and grabbed a star and threw it into my eye. The light woke me up out of my sleep.

From that day on I had double vision just like God had said. My visions were more revealing than ever. Before I would dream of a male and it would be a female. I would dream of a person, but it would be someone else. My dreams had become specific to where they were almost an instant revelation. Once I dreamed about my daughter's aunt's car. In the dream I had somehow became responsible for her car and I lost it. So I went everywhere inquiring about this black car. The day before the dream I had a conversation with her on the phone and in the dream I began to cry. I was asking myself why I didn't mention the car to her then. When I woke up from this dream, I was still crying and I couldn't stop. I called her to make sure everything was ok. Later that week she called me and told me that she was in a car accident. I didn't think about the dream that I had at that point. She said that she was all right. One week after having this dream, she called me to tell me that she was in pain and asked me to take her to the hospital. I told her that I would be right over. When I pulled up I saw her car in the parking lot damaged and I immediately went back to my dream about the black car. This was just the beginning of the elevation that *Getting Back Up* had taken place and how my dreams would be a way for God to communicate with me.

I called my aunt almost every other day and went to see her as often as I could. When she saw things in my life, I was seeing things in her life. I felt like she would need help financially from time to time and I was more than glad to help. This became a habit that was almost as devastating as the use of narcotics. God said that you should have no God before him. Me being who I was got it all confused and I began to worship her. It didn't take long for God to reveal to me that she was just a person. This was another person that he had chosen to use. She had personality flaws just like me and God was using her. I think the whole relationship was to show me this. God uses whom ever he wants for his Glory. When he feels that he is not getting the Glory he'll move people from your life with quickness. One day she just turned on me and I couldn't understand why.

I immediately reverted back to type. I thought of the many times that I went out of my way for her and how she didn't appreciate it one bit. As a matter of fact, she became really comfortable and I was starting to feel used. I learned how to love her as my aunt, but still this relationship was severed and I was so heart broken. It reminded me of how I felt when I was in the street. When I smoked crack my mouth would twist and I couldn't speak, but somehow things always got twisted and I was misunderstood. I would always end up in some kind of confusion. Well a confusion spirit came between the two of us. Something like the temple of Babel. The last thing that she told me was that God told her not to tell me anything else. She told me that God told her that he would tell me himself.

When we stopped communicating, God started talking to me. This let me know that he was ever by my side and I could no longer worry about what people said, felt or thought. God was truly in control of my life. I still struggle with the fact that people who are so connected, faithfully going to church and all, could act the way they did towards me and other people. I found out that as long as we are wrapped in this flesh we are not perfection and that is why we need the Lord, Jesus. I was learning more and more about God. I'd turn on the ministers in the morning and in the evening. I wanted to hear from God everyday and I found out that I didn't need any one specific person to hear from him. I could hear from God in dreams. I could hear from God through his word. I could even hear from God in the people that I would talk to or pass on the street. I was able to find God everywhere that I sought him. I was grateful for the anointing that I was walking in, however, I soon found out that to whom much is given much is required. I learned about the huge responsibility that comes with the gift that God had planted inside. This put in me touched with the fact that if he could hide such a precious thing inside of me, who is unworthy, undeserving and inexperienced, then he could hide treasures in all of us. I learned that our gifts came without repentance. But then came a huge responsibility and that was learning how to walk in the gift. I found out that everyone has at least one gift. Among these gifts God gave to every man free will. I found out that not everyone would use his or her gift to the Glory of the Lord. I found out that sometimes flesh got in the way and sometimes we as people wanted glory for ourselves. And, finally, I found out that Satan was after the gift. When I heard that Satan came to steal, kill and destroy. I realized that the anointing was really what he was after. The closer that I got to God the bigger Satan appeared to be. I don't dare say who is gifted and who is not. I don't dare say who is anointed and who is not. But, today I thank God for the anointing and I thank God for his word. The word of God makes the difference. With the word I am able to discern those things, which are of God, and, those things, which are of the flesh. I was more and more excited with each revelation, but then I found myself more heart broken and discouraged. This walk with the Lord was not getting any easier. That is because, by nature, I complicate everything. I was seeing some things supematurally, and I was afraid. I was afraid of my aunt whom I know today is a Prophetess and not just some Psychic. I was afraid of people laying their hands on me. I was afraid of the anointing oil. To me the whole thing resembled witchcraft. I needed answers and the Holy Spirit taught me.

In times like these people have to believe in something. We want to believe that life has some plan or purpose and that we're not just out there floating in space aimlessly. In other words God or the Creator didn't just leave us here on this planet to suffer and then die. The desire to feel guided, protected, comforted, and loved unconditionally are human conditions that humans don't have the capacity to give other humans. So most of us believe in a greater being. Billions of people believe in God. Out of mass majority we have Christians, Muslims, Jews, Masons and a whole host of other religions that believe in the one true God. Christians represent about fifty percent of the "One True God Believers." Out of the large number of Christians there are still several differences in the way we worship, live and believe. Christianity was founded sometime shortly after the death of Christ and it has changed tremendously since then. We as Christians believe that Christ died for our sins and that through him we have the gift of eternal life, (John 3:16), but prior to the birth and death of Christ, there were always people who believed in this One God who had infinite wisdom and power. So, just as we believe that our God possess infinite power, there is another group that believes that the Prince of Darkness, Satan, possess equal power in the universe. There is a very thin line between Spiritual Warfare and Witchcraft.

When I was a child, growing up in this society I was conditioned to desire instant gratification. I watch "Bewitched" and "I Dream of Jeannie." They were sitcoms that I grew up on and I had the idea that I could blink and get what ever I wanted. Until later when I found out that it didn't quite work like that, and if it did it probably was witchcraft. I was taught that things don't happen overnight, and that money doesn't grow on trees. Then I was introduced to the Lord Jesus. I listened as people witnessed about the power of the Holy Ghost. So there is a large mass of people walking around believing that if we only ask in the name of Jesus, and believe, then it shall come to pass. And it is true! Where are the lines really drawn between right and wrong, black and white or Witchcraft and Warfare? Now there is a modem day religion for witches. I've read that they have three types of witches. White witches, Black Witches and Grey Witches. These colors separate the difference and the practices of the so-called witches.

Now, in the church we are doing something really similar to witchcraft. What is the difference between casting a spell and saying a prayer? If witches have a breakdown between good and bad, then how do we discern a prayer, which is good from a good incantation? It is my understanding that for everything that God created, Satan made a counterfeit. So just as Satan and his army have powers, we as God's children also possess power through the Lord Jesus. Because God is Alpha and Omega (Rev. 22:13), then God would have had to possess the power first. The original is always more powerful than the counterfeit. Remember when Moses and Pharaoh had a showdown. God told Aaron who was with Moses to cast down the rod. Aaron cast down the rod before Pharaoh and it turned into a serpent. Then Pharaoh commanded the magicians, sorcerers and wise men to cast down their rods and they became serpents also. The serpent that Aaron had, being more powerful, swallowed up all of the other serpents, (Exodus 7:10-12). I have become aware of the fact that there is a spiritual war going on inside this world and in the heavens. We can't see these forces with our naked eye and because the war is spiritual, we need spiritual weapons to fight. The only weapon we have is the word of God. When God created man in his image, what he did was give man the capacity to speak a thing into existence. The Bible says that Christ called those things that be not as though they were. Just like in the beginning when God created the whole universe by a spoken word. God said, "Let there be..." and the universe obeyed God's word, (Genesis 1:3-26).

We as Christians should be careful of the invisible line between good and evil. We need to be sure about whom we believe and what we're believing for. Satan's whole purpose is to deceive the whole world and he is gaining in numbers just by counting the so-called saints.

There are a lot of saints who don't know who it is they are summonsing through prayer. There are evil spirits around that will simply grant your wishes. Satan promised Jesus the whole world, (Luke 4:5-6). This means that Satan can give gifts and disguise them as blessings. So how do we know? How do we check a blessing out? Do we really need to be so careful or does God know what we mean? God does know our hearts, (1st Samuel 16:7). He knows our heart better than we do. So we don't always know our motives for the things we request of the Lord. We act out of our shortsightedness and out of our immediate need. And in the same day we said that the Lord would supply all of our needs according to his riches in Glory, (Phil. 4:19), if so then why do we have to pray for our needs?

Think about it. Most of the things that we pray for are things that we want, not the things we need. Some times we get bold. We go as far as to pray for our desire for someone else's life. So it becomes our will not thy will be done. This is a very sensitive topic. Everyone believes that they are doing the right thing and saying the right thing by talking to our father and asking him for what we desire. The Bible says that if we delight ourselves in the Lord, he will give us the desires of our hearts, (Psalm 37:4). Again, we don't really know what's in our hearts, do we, (1st Kings 8:38-39)? The Bible says to seek ye first the kingdom of God and his righteousness, (Matt 6:33). I believe that is the one piece of information that is key. If we followed this one guideline it would be hard to get distracted. If we sought and found the kingdom, that would leave little room for error. We would dwell in the house of the Lord. We know that evil is not present in the house of the Lord.

God cast Satan and a third of the angels out of heaven. Do you think that they just went and sat down somewhere? No, not hardly. Satan and these angels still believe that they are just as powerful as God. So they are hanging out in the earth. They are at the playground, in our homes and in our churches.

Our Holy Bible makes suggestions, gives guidelines, and then there are spiritual laws that God has put in place to govern this universe. There are procedures and instructions for obtaining peace in one's life and there are promises that God made to each one of his children. Out of all of God's promises, instructions, guidelines, procedures, and suggestions, remember that we all have free will. We have a choice and minute-by-minute we are choosing. We are choosing good or evil while good and evil are in a constant war for our souls; however, good and evil have to obey spiritual laws.

We as people are somewhat limited to something called human nature. We as Christians call it "the flesh." Our flesh and the desires of the flesh are a direct influence on our choices and the things we choose for our life. Sometimes, we make the wrong choice based on something we consider to be an immediate need. Truthfully, we really don't know what we need and the things we want we don't know if it's good for us or not. That is why we need guidance from the Lord in every matter. He is concerned about every aspect of our lives. He knows the beginning and he knows the very thing that will cause our demise. This is why complete dependence on the Lord Jesus is significant.

While we are in the flesh we are rendered powerless. We are powerless over sickness and disease, we are powerless over strongholds and addictions, and we are powerless over other people and situations in our lives. But God the Father has power over all of these things, and as his children, we have access to this power, but only through the Lord Jesus. That is why we must have a personal relationship with Him.

One of the spiritual laws is "as a man thinketh in his heart so shall it be." Imagine how dangerous our prayers can be if we do not really know the Lord Jesus. God set forth his laws in the beginning and it shall remain unto the end. God doesn't change his mind so we can know for sure that when he made this law, it remains in the universe. Knowing that we would mess up and make mistakes and put other things before him, he put us first and set in place a law that the whole universe would have to obey. Even He. So blessings can fall on the just as well as the unjust. And if the unrighteous declare a thing, and believe this thing in his heart, there is a good chance that this thing will come to pass. We have some advantages as Christians. For one thing the Bible says that the prayers of the righteous availeth much, (James 5:16). It may appear that Satan and his followers are very powerful in the Earth, but they can't move anything in the Heaven. The one thing that should concern us as Christian's should be salvation. This is the only thing that promises us eternal life. This surpasses anything that we may ask. The word of God says that he is able to do exceedingly and abundantly above all that we may ask or think, (Ephesians 3:20). We can't imagine life eternal, we can't possibly imagine a world without sickness or death and we can't even begin to think of living without our bodies (flesh). So this very thing can cause us to lean in the direction of instant gratification. Jesus said that he came that we might have life and have it more abundantly (John 10:10). So this justifies our tendency to pray for things and to expect them right away.

Anything that is worth having is worth waiting for. Remember Sarah and Abraham. God told them that they would have a son. They figured that because of their age they could not have a baby. So they tried to help God out. Sarah went to Hagar, the slave woman, and told her to sleep with her husband, Abraham and to have a son for them. This was not what God told her to do, but in her limited understanding she figured that she knew what to do. This child conceived out of adultery had grown to almost a man before the promised seed came forth, (Genesis 18:10). Another scenario is King David, (II Samuel 2:7), God anointed him king about seventeen years before he sat on the throne. While God is blessing someone, he has the whole world in mind and we know that all things work together for good for those who love God and who are called according to his purpose, (Romans 8:28).

Gladys is a Christian. She professes the Lord Jesus as her personal savior. God has brought her through all kinds of hell and is still bringing her through. Miss Holy sanctified notices that Gladys is doing something that is not considered Christian-like and she makes up her mind at that point that she is the one who will point it out and she is the one who will correct this. She goes over to

Gladys and tells her "God told me to tell you this... Let's pray." Miss Holy Sanctified starts to pray for her will to be done in Gladys' life. Gladys, feeling inferior trusts that God really did speak to this person and she agrees. "Amen." Immediately, Gladys feels that God is mad at her. "He must be, he didn't tell me that." So Gladys, who is not on the same level as Miss Holy- Sanctified, starts to feel pressured to please this person who took it upon herself to chastise her. Gladys immediately proceeds to work on this unacceptable area of her life, but failed. This caused her to run away from the church. Christians make this mistake all of the time. Gladys' mistake is giving this power to another person and allowing her to make her feel inferior. Miss Holy Sanctified's mistake was to judge Gladys, (Matt.7: 1-3) and her other mistake was to cause this person to turn away from the church, (Matt. 18:6). I would certainly turn away from a God who has turned away from me.

Can you see how Satan can use Christians to turn other Christians away from God? He can deceive you into believing that you are capable of correcting a certain area on your own without the help of the most-high God. He can deceive you into believing that someone else is perfect thus being more loved by God than you. He can deceive you into believing that you cannot come to God unless you're perfect; that we somehow merit the blessings of God. There are a lot of people who are still trying to pay for salvation. If we had to make this purchase again then Lord Jesus lived and died in vain. Satan can cause some folks to believe that they possess the power to change people, and really what they are doing is going around casting spells on people while ultimately forgetting to examine themselves. Satan can have you so focused on someone else's faults that you can forget that you too have faults. Can you imagine walking around judging everyone and on your way to Hell? Remember, vanity was the sin that got Satan and one third of the angels cast out from heaven.

Touching and agreeing can be dangerous for both people. If the person that is praying is asking for their will for your life, you could be agreeing to something outside of the will of God. Suppose they are speaking in tongues. If you do not have the gift of speaking and translating tongues, you have no idea what they are speaking into your life. We say Amen in agreement and this acts as some kind of approval stamp placed on a prayer we know nothing about. God's word doesn't return unto him void. So if you touch and agree in the name of Jesus you had better know who you are touching and what you are requesting. Spirits are transferable. Remember the man "Legion" and how his demons were cast into the pigs, (Luke 8:27-33)? Witches often use contact to cast spells on people. If you see someone and you want to lay hands on them, if you're not truly appointed and anointed to do so, it is important to remember that demons can transfer. In Ephesians 4:1 it tells us that you should walk worthy of the vocation wherewith you are called. If you see something that someone is doing wrong, it may help to examine yourself first. Ask God why their problem is such a distraction for you? You'll be amazed at the answer.

How do you know? Once you have a relationship with Jesus, and talk to him on a regular basis. He will talk back. He will give you the spirit of discernment. This is a vital tool. This will keep you out of a lot of trouble. Learn how to listen when your spirit is talking to you. God gave angels charge over you to keep you in all your ways (Psalms 91:11), and, God said in 1st Corinthians 12:1 that he will not have you ignorant concerning spiritual gifts. Ask God to give you a prayer partner, someone that you can pray with on a regular basis. You will get to know each other by the spirit.

God say that his sheep know his voice, (John 10:4). So once God speaks to you about a certain thing, first you and your prayer partner should go to God and give thanks for all that he has already done. Then the two of you can agree that you will have revelation of his will for you life. Another spiritual law is that when praises go up, blessings come down. Don't forget to praise God. This is very important because it puts God in his rightful place and that's first place. God love's to know that he comes first. He made that his first commandment. Remember that an instant anointing may be a brand of witchcraft. When Jesus comes for the church I want to hear him say, "Well done;" I'm sure that no one wants to hear the words "Depart from me for I know you not." Among the different groups of Christians, about one third don't believe in the rapture, one third believe that we will live through the tribulation and the rest believe that God will come and receive his church before this dreadful time. As Christians, we have more similarities to witches, warlocks, and satanic worshippers than we have with the different groups among our fellow Christians. It is no coincidence that the ties that bind us together seems to be weaker than those that separate us. This is a trick of the enemy.

Satan wants us to go around and act as if we're defeated, wilderness wanderers who simply got tired of waiting on God and decided to take things into our own hands.

Remember, easy come, easy go. Isaiah says those who wait on the lord will mount up with wings like an eagle and shall renew their strength. (Isaiah 40:31) Be willing to wait and trust that the things you need you already have and the things you want are on the way as long as God is in his rightful place. Just think of a radio. There is a cord and a place for the batteries. We can select on this radio (DC) direct current, which tells us that the source of power will come from the battery. Then we have the alternate current (AC), which tells us that the source of power is going to come from a connection, thus being the cord.

Let's say that God is this energy; He represents the Electric Company and you are the communication device, the radio. Let's imagine that the cord is the Word of God, the connection, and the Holy Ghost is the on/off button, access. We know that there is a price to run this energy into the communication device but we will never receive the bill because Jesus paid all of the bills past, present and future, authorization. Now imagine the same radio that is running on a counterfeit, the battery. If you are hooked up using an alternate current you can turn on this power at any time and if you turn it off the energy will still be there when you're ready to connect again. But I promise you that if you use a battery, it will surely die. So if we are hooked up to the source, God. By the authorization of Jesus who paid it all, and connected by the word of God and we have access to the revelation by turning on the Holy spirit, then yes, we have infinite power. However, if we want to stray from the house of the Lord we would have to use a direct current, the battery. And as long as we are willing to buy batteries we can possess this power. There is a very high price to pay for using this power. Remember that there are supernatural forces in the earth and they may possess power, but God is the one true source of power in the universe and for access Jesus paid it all.

Chapter Fourteen

THE DREAMER

I was quite the dreamer for a while and my dreams were full of revelation. I couldn't wait to share these dreams with people when I was awake and even though they needed no translation, I still wanted and invited everyone's opinion. 'What do you think God meant by that?" I found out that some of my visions would continue to reveal themselves in my life long after the dream was over. I was finding out about the timing of God. I realized that God is the same yesterday, today and forever. I found out that the past, present and future was all one with God and that time was something that man measured and treasured more than God. I would have to learn how to wait on him. Once I had a vision and shared it with everyone, I thought that my next thing was to act. I would do the right thing at the wrong time. I didn't know how to wait on God. Most of the time He was revealing the work that he would do required me to do nothing. The revelation was just to prepare me for the blessing to come and I had no more power than I had before the vision.

Some dreams were for me and not everyone else. I opened my life so wide for everyone. This damaged me and my faith because the more I let people in my life and received their opinion about me the more I saw my inadequacies. I was already a victim of low self-esteem and I allowed the enemy to use people to accomplish what he had set out to do in my life. I dreamed once that I was watching Christian television with my mother. I didn't see her face, but I felt her presence with me. I saw a young lady on the television that looked like me and she was preaching. I was talking to her "look Ma, that girl she looks like me. Is that me, ma?" I felt that this meant that I would evangelize one day, however, this would have to be in God's time. I'm sure glad that I didn't run to the television station and grab a microphone that day. One night I was in bed sleeping and I had left Christian television on. I dreamed that I woke up and I felt an evil presence. Just what the old folks in my family used to call "witch riding." I felt bounded and I started to pray. Once I prayed I was able to move and I headed for the door to my bedroom. I saw myself lying in a fetal position and evil was all around me. I saw a big black shadow like being and a black cat surrounding my body on the floor. I tried to get near my body and the cat threw his back up and screeched at me. I had someone to translate and they said that it was my flesh dying. Shortly after that I had company over for the weekend and they were praying, just ushering in the spirit of the Lord. I ended up in those dark clothes, laying in the fetal position and answering a call to ministry. I remember promising God that I would tell it. I would tell it. I was at work one day and a young African woman told me that I was going to preach. She told me to get ready. I asked her "how do you get ready for that?" She told me that I'd walk into it. This was another incident that let me know that God has a time for everything. I just didn't understand how God could use me for such when I was so messed up in my flesh, but what I did understand was that there would be a process and God would have to do it because I couldn't.

Meanwhile, I would share these visions with people and they would dismiss every word. I could still hear them saying "Why would God use you to preach, when he has me, The Saint. You don't even go to church." I was on a roller coaster. God would lift me up by night and people would tear me down by day. I had another vision once. I dreamed that my boss had offered me another position on the job. I loved the job that I was in and I seemed reluctant in the dream to accept the job. When I woke up I understood that this would mean a promotion. I thanked the Lord for the promotion even though there was really no upward mobility in the job that I was doing. I was as far as I could go. I worked for the Vice President of a large company. My title was Administrative Assistant. What was the next step? I had no idea what God had in store for me. I had even less of an idea what Satan would do. The next day I was at work and near the end of the day, I was asked to find about three hundred chairs. We were having a big meeting the next morning and this was not a request, this was a demand. I called around to several party shops and finally found the chairs. By 4:00 that afternoon, the chairs were there and we were setting them up. I was doing my very best since I believed that I would get this promotion. I went home that evening wondering what in the world could this big meeting be about. Normally I would have this information before anyone, being right next to the big boss. She didn't even offer up a clue as to the importance of the meeting. In my mind this definitely confirmed one thing and that was that things in my work place were definitely going to change.

The next morning I rushed to work to find out what the meeting was about. It was a meeting announcing that we would start outsourcing. While the Senior Vice President gave us every confidence that this would not affect our jobs, everyone there was affected at some point. The devil had planned and attack for me though. They had announced a new unit which would open up about ten or more positions. I paid that announcement no attention at all. I folded up the chairs after the meeting, waited for the company to come and pick them up and I knew no more about this so-called promotion than I did the day before. I received a call from one of the employees and she was asking me about one of the jobs that they had announced at the meeting. I didn't know what she was talking about. I looked down and I saw some staffing requisitions that I would process the next day. I thought to myself "this is what she is talking about." She continued, "How much does that position pay?" I told her I didn't know, but I gave her a range. This was a corporate sin. I had disclosed confidential information. I didn't realize that this was a trap. I called my boss before leaving to ask if there was anything she needed before I left for the day and she was not in her office. I did a last walk around to make sure everything was in place before leaving. I found my boss at the woman's desk that I was just speaking with. Damn, I had been set up. The next morning I was called into my boss's office and the only thing I knew for sure was that God was about to reveal that promotion dream to me. When I sat down she started in on me right away. "I could fire your ass right now" She proceeded to tell me that she was not happy with the way that I had handled confidential information. She told me that maybe this is not the job for me. She told me that I could have another job in the department. I knew that the enemy had set me up and I was crushed. I didn't even try to defend myself because I noticed that over her head there was a big hand and in this hand was a spear. Right then God had showed me that he had stopped the arrow that the enemy had aimed at my job. I was grateful that I didn't lose my job and I was thinking about reluctantly accepting another position. I feared my boss and I felt that in spite of all of my efforts to please her, she would do me in. Now she didn't trust me and I knew that this would make things very difficult. I was so upset. I had the following day off and when I returned I saw God starting to move. My boss asked me to call and check on our incentives. Knowing that she gets them from more than one location, I asked her where did she place the order. Her reply was "Straight off the streets of DC." So I thought to myself, "Does this mean Greenbelt." I walked away looking puzzled. Just then, she called me back into her office and she told me that someone had gone out on our message boards and trashed her name. I didn't have any idea about what was going on and at that moment she recognized this. Our relationship began to change.

She was going to fire me and within days she was under a much bigger attack. I began to pray for her and

I wrote her a letter of encouragement. I explained to her that the house was under attack. She fully received what I was saying to her. Not only that she seemed to trust me again but eventually she left.

God warned me of an attack, he kept that formed weapon from prospering and then he showed me his salvation. I stayed on this job and I was still convinced that God meant promotion. I never even realized that he had already promoted me spiritually. I thought about the Hebrew boys and how they were promoted right after coming from the fire. I was so grateful.

It appeared that I was holding the whole team together once she left and I was sure then that I was moving up in my career. I found out that she had left, but Satan was still very present and the pressure that I was under on this job was about to kill me. Finally, they hired another VP. I was excited and I just knew that he would be better than my first boss. The Senior Vice President told me to clean his office and I did to the best of my ability. I went into the office and I blessed the desk, the chairs, the walls and floors in Jesus name. I had no idea that I was preparing this office for Satan. The anointing that was in his office made him uncomfortable from the very beginning and he made that clear to me upon our first meeting. He told me that he knew that I wasn't going to meet his standards because his office wasn't clean. Needless to say, what I had believed to be a revelation about a promotion on my job was a warning and eventually I would have to leave.

It was in this situation that I realized the revelation that God had given me prior to all of this. This time

I wasn't asleep. I was standing in the bathroom mirror curling my hair and God told me "Triple by-pass." I answered God "there is nothing wrong with my heart." He answered me and said "Why did you bring it to me?" Then God started showing me the operation. He showed me my heart and he continued to speak. Where you are expecting your job to provide for you, I am going to hook you up with Jehovah Jirah, for Jesus, the son of God will be my provider. Where you expect your grandparents to keep you, I am going to hook you up to the Holy Spirit, for he will keep thee in all thy ways. Lastly, God showed me a main artery and he told me that where I was hooked up with men and I expected them to love me, when they didn't I was non functional. There was a major blockage and God told me that he would hook me up to God the Father. I was so happy to hear from God that morning. I was crying the night before, but God had brought me joy that morning. Just hearing his voice was enough to fill me up in empty places, but then I realized that God meant surgery. I told God "but that's going to hurt." And it was starting to hurt really bad. I had shared this dream with a man and he told me that the fact that I was awake when God gave me this revelation meant that God was not giving me any anesthesia.

Now I had been in surgery for several months and I didn't even realize that I was in surgery just like God said. He was already working in the area of my job. I found a job paying more money and I left my position. On my new job, I was in a very small office with five people. A neurotic, a harlot, a homosexual, a drug addict and a Jehovah's witness. I struggled. I had no tolerance for these people. Somehow I was better than they. He severed me from that job and showed me how he could provide for me. After several months and not finding anything, I prayed to God about finding a job and God told me, "If I told you that I was going to take care of you for a little while, how would you feel?" I told God that I would be grinning. Well, that is exactly what he did. My bills were paid while I was out of work. He truly showed me that I must depend on Jesus and not a job. The second part of that revelation had to do with my grandparents who are wonderful care giving individuals. They took care of my mother, they took care of my sister and me, and now they were taking care of my kids. They wouldn't have it any other way. But my dependency on them was so much so that I would have nightmares about one of them dying and leaving me. I was petrified. I would call them three to four times a day, and everyday that I was able to hear their voice again made me glad that they were still there. It made me feel secure. But the more closer I got to Jesus, I found out that my love for them was controlling my whole life and that God will not have gods before him. My life did not belong to them, my life belonged to God. God started requiring me to do things like raise my children. This seemed reasonable, but my grandparents were not trying to have it. So I struggled with the dilemma. Who should I please? My children stayed with them during the week. This part of the procedure is probably the hardest because it caused me to compromise. I realized that the spiritual aspect is always the hardest because my flesh, which is tangible, is being hooked up to a Spirit, which is not tangible. So I can tell you today that I know God was working this thing out although I had no idea how. And the last part of the revelation, "the men" and how God wanted to have me hooked up with him first. But I was already in a relationship that I thought was the best that I had ever been in. This would mean sacrifice. The biggest sacrafice that I had ever made. I was married and one day my husband and I separated. I never got a divorce and I rationalized this by saying that I was never married. I saw no wrong in my current relationship because it was not abusi ve. But God started snatching the covers off of this individual and the relationship became devastating to me. I started having visions from God immediately about this relationship, but I couldn't see anything wrong with my natural eye. I kept justifying. I told God "He doesn't run the street, he doesn't cheat and he doesn't drink." God revealed to me that he would do all three. This was so devastating to me, but when God showed me, I let this man go. I suffered so badly. There wasn't a minute that I wasn't thinking of him during the day and at night my flesh longed for him. I cried almost every night and everyday. Meanwhile, just as the prophet had told me, my husband came back around. He visited a few times and it was spiritual. He told me that he knew that he wasn't living right. He told me that I was his wife. He told me that he knew God wanted to use him, and the best part of all is that he told me he was sorry. A few weeks later he had been killed. This was such a shock to me because I thought that God had severed the other relationship so that he could give me back my husband. I knew that it would take time, a long time because I was no longer in love with this man. But what God revealed through this is that one time I was totally dependant on him and eventually all of that hurt went away. I would have to trust that He is the same God that delivered me from that abuse, He was the same God that delivered me from crack and that he would one day deliver me from the man that I was so much in love with currently. I missed that point also.

I felt like when God took my husband home, it meant that it was ok to go back to the man I love, and I did. I thought that while we were separated somehow things had gotten better. When we got back together God was still revealing things to me about this man. Not only was he going out, he was going to strip bars. Not only was he drinking, he was smoking marijuana again, and not only was he seeing someone else, she was a white woman. This seems to be the "Are you really a strong black woman test of the century." I wanted to die. I never had a problem with interracial relationships before but I found out that as long as it wasn't me, I could handle it. The truth of the matter was that it made me feel less than. I felt like I was less of a woman. Was I that horrible to cause a man to abandon his race? Hell No! Men that do this have their own set of issues and the white women as well. For hundreds of years they weren't allowed to even look at each other, so being human, we always desire what we can't have. I desired him and God told me that I couldn't have him so I was just as guilty of being this human. Even though he was back in my life I couldn't get over what God had showed me. I figured if I was with this man all of these years and I couldn 't see any of this in him, how could I be sure that these things would not continue. I couldn't be. My only sure thing at this point was the Lord, Jesus Christ as I remain on the operating table until God would complete this procedure. During this time I wrote about the pain that I was in and I came up with some pretty interesting poetry.

Chapter Fifteen

POETRY

BLACK WOMAN, CHOOSE

You're in a relationship just you and your king
And for some reason it doesn't feel right
You are in charge of everything
And the king ends up with a woman that's white.

Over and over you process this thing
Was I good enough; what did I do?
Maybe your man was not a king
Maybe he did not belong with you

Your life became an endless night
You walk around in darkness looking for day
It seems as though nothing is right
But then you realize you threw him away

Just like a mother who gives away a child
You hear them crying, calling to you in your sleep
You start to remember the wonderful smile
Of the child that you chose not to keep

"Give him back to me; a birthmother has the right
The law says so, and for my king, I am going to fight
You don't know how to raise a black king
How could you know, you're white"

And your king just stands there watching
As his self esteem has risen
Never realizing that what he found
Is just another prison

For once in his life, he's got it made
He imagine his skin a lighter shade
He enjoys the things they do
But then he remembers loving you

He remembers the nurturing with a soft twist of wrath
He remembers when he was dirty; you gave his flesh a bath
He remembers when he was down and you picked him up
Placed your breast inside his mouth and he began to suck

Oh he remembers his queen now
He remembers lying up in your womb
But that was no place for a king
So it became his tomb

He remembers the comfort that you provided in the home
But when you threw your king away, he decides to roam
You ask yourself, "Would I feel this
way, if she were only black?
But since she's white your heart is fixed
on getting this man back

Don't feel bad that she picked him
up; be glad that it was she
It could have been a whole lot worse;
she could have been a he
So finally you've found him and you feel like you have won
You feel superficially fulfilled because
you have claimed your son

So, has he grown any since he has been away?
Or changed any habits since you let him out to play?
Or is he just the same, as before you both got free?
If so; let her have him, she can afford the therapy

The issue is not black or white; right or wrong; win or lose
The fact is that we have a choice and we simply must choose
We have a choice to be Queen or
Mom; its one job or the other
Only a King deserves a queen, a boy deserves his mother

BUT HE TOLD ME NO

Have you ever loved someone with all of you heart?
The more you seem to try; things just fall apart
You rationalize the way they treat you and
promise yourself "they'll change"
Your focus on them is so much that
your vision has been deranged

Where truth used to be your friend; you
run and hide your shameful face
And you try to deal with the hurt you
feel in a very sad and lonely place
You ask yourself if there were any signs
that said "Quick Sand Ahead"
And you remember yes there was, but
it's too late for that I'm dead!

Why didn't my father stop me? Why did he let me go?
But my father whispered to me and said
"Remember, I told you NO!
"I gave you the desire of your heart just so you could see
That no man can love you until he comes through me
But what you must do is set apart,
what is flesh, what is heart

Do not partake of evil or compromise in any way
Do not go on Satan's playground, he does not wish to play
He comes only seeking whom ever he can devour
And you can be victorious, but you give away your power"
"Sometimes I will cut you back so that you will grow

But as a loving parent sometimes I must tell you NO
I know where I am taking you; for I can see the end
But you go around in circles because
you choose to worship men
And yet you call to me "Father, please bless my friend"
Give me your broken heart I will mend it again and again
Soon you will learn that Satan cannot be your friend
I know what's best for you; I know just what you need
But you must have the faith the size of a mustard seed
You must worship in spirit do not let flesh lead
You must place your trust in me or you will not succeed"

Seek ye first the kingdom and let my father do the rest
You are his loving children and I think he knows what's best
I want to live and prosper' I want my faith to grow
I want to learn to listen when my father tells me no

These are some of the things that I was writing while going through this great tribulation and this surgery that I am starting to take very seriously. I don't give myself too much credit for the things that have taken place. I just know that there is a reason for everything and while I ride I just sit back and learn more every day. I am learning about the goodness of God. I learn that God never forces us to do anything. So, I am required to do something and that is to choose him daily. No matter what the circumstances, no matter what I'm going through, I am learning how to lean on the Lord, Jesus. I'm finding out even today what disobedience cost me. And now as I lay on the table bleeding from the heart, my master comforts me and says "I am not finished with you yet." He is still very much in love with me. He is still blessing me and he constantly reminds me that there is no condemnation to those who are in Christ Jesus. He reminds me that all things work together for good for those who love God and are called according to his purpose. He assures me that He is still God and that Satan is still a liar.

SATAN YOU'RE A LIAR 11

You've tried to kill me with abuse
But it was to no avail
And then you sent your Demon Crack
To bring me straight to hell

But God has brought me through all that
He extinguished your dreadful fire
And now you send the bigger imps
But, Satan you're a liar

Well, I've grown a little
Since you and I last talked
Through Jesus I have learned to crawl
And then I learned to walk

I hear you calling me crack head
That used to be my name
Telling me that I should be dead
That I should be ashamed

I hear you calling me prostitute
But, no more, not for you
You see now that I'm all sold out
For Jesus who is true

You try to use my loved ones
To keep me in the grips
And make me curse the ones I love
By using my holy lips

You try to seduce me with anger
And cause my flesh to rise
And then you make me feel real bad
With all your horrible lies

You set people in my pathway
Whom you've disguised as friends
They try to discourage me
But they will never win

People that try to make me believe
That God has left my side
But I know my God is with me
And in him I do abide.

Even though I fall sometimes
Into your dreadful plan
My father is ever forgiving me
And has kept me in his hand

Satan, you have lost me
And let me tell you why
Because you never tell the truth
And my God can never lie

I know now why you hate me
I have inherited your seat

I notice how adamant you are
To never admit defeat

I know that you are afraid of me
Because you know I'll tell it now
And when the truth shall hit the streets
I'll turn hell upside down

I'm going to tell the world about Jesus
About his mercy and his grace
That no matter how far down they've gone
That they can always seek his face

And then I'll tell these sinners
How I was about to die
Simply because I entertained you
The author of all lies

I am glad I met the lord
Even under your attack
Because I now believe his word
I'm never turning back

I won't even try to fight you
Because my God is more equipped
He'll send the angel Michael
So his baby don't get whipped

Even though I'm no match for you
In Christ I'm climbing higher
I'm finding strength to resist you now
For my soul is your desire

Chapter Sixteen

HANGING FROM THE TWELFTH STEP

It was in the winter of 1999 and 2000 when God told me to start writing. I had no idea that He was going to write the book. He allowed me to reflect on some of the most painful things in my life. He showed me how he has always been there. I was very much in touched with the realization that I should have been dead. I should have hung on the cross and died for my sins, not Christ. But, not one drop of my blood had redemption power in it. God told me to write and he locked me in for the first weekend with a snowstorm. I was able to focus on the pain. I had a very painful life and most of it was my own fault. He showed me that I could stay in misery as long as I chose to. I earned that right. But he showed me that through his grace and mercy, that I could be set free totally. Not just free from drugs. I found out that with addiction traveled a host of other demonic entities. And there I was standing with the weight of a legion on my back. God was showing me that when ever I was ready that I could just lay them all down. Then I found out that the transformation from addict to recovery was a short trip. That was nothing compared to what God would do in me. This was very painful for me. It had to be. My flesh was dying. But this time, I was in touched with the fact that there was no part of me that was worth salvation. That I really didn't deserve to live. God showed me my pain and told me that he would now change my life. It sounded good, but this was very painful. Painful to experience, painful to observe, painful to write about, but God was making me over and there wasn't a thing that I could do about it. I had already said yes to Jesus. I wanted him to change the very ugly things that I saw in myself and hated about Tammy. But, God started tapping into even the things that I loved about Tammy. This is where resistance came in and I fought to save the last little bits of myself. For they were what defined who I was. Never think that you will come to Christ and remain the way you were. God is not a man that he should lie. When God told me that he would change everything. I was willing. I just didn't have the capacity to determine what everything was. And the thought of turning back is not an option, because when I looked back again all I saw was the cross.

So I carried to message to other addicts. Letting them know that they never had to use drugs again. Trying to be an example. So can you tell me why I couldn't save my boyfriend? Could you tell me why I was so miserable in my eighth year of recovery?

I was almost used to the fact that my lover and I was at the end. I only needed time to separate myself emotionally from him. The drinking never stopped, I just got used to it. So used to it that it was in my refrigerator and I would be comfortable with the fact that it would go and he right behind it. I had accepted the fact that I shouldn't have gone out to retrieve my heartache. If God wanted us together then he would do it. I was powerless and I was comfortable with powerlessness. I couldn't change anyone. I was realizing this and the fact that I couldn't even change me.

I stepped outside of my comfort zone and moved into a townhouse that was way above my means. This is what we called a geographical cure. I was subleasing from my cousin. She changed her mind and I had to move within four months. I had just started another job and after a week, they told us that they were relocating. The devastation of the situations around me caused me to break. I found out then that I was pregnant with a third child. The blessing was that God gave me a chance to go through a pregnancy sober, well, without a drug or drink.

I was miserable as every part of my life was turned upside down. Now more than ever I would have to learn to depend on God. But let me tell you, while I was living in sin with this man, I was scared to go to God and ask him to help me. This misconception kept me in sickness all of my life. While I was smoking crack, God loved me. I couldn't understand why after being clean so long, I was still sick.

So, then I was having a baby! I was fighting with my boyfriend everyday. I had a best friend and she was with me when I found out that I was pregnant. There was nothing that I wouldn't do for her. At the time I discovered my pregnancy, I was unemployed again and at the end of my severance package that God gracefully gave me. She asked me for a loan and I loaned her money to pay her rent. I never saw her again. This broke my heart. I remember witnessing to her one day. We prayed. We read the word. I was sharing with her about the fact that if we ask God a question and then read his word that he would reveal an answer. She wanted to test this immediately. Ask God when will I find a job? So I asked God and God sent me to Proverbs and told me to "guard my heart because out of it came the issues of life." I was looking for her answer and God spoke to me. This taught me to go to God on my behalf. I was no one's savior. It took a while for the revelation to catch up with the word of God and there I was with no money and my friend was gone. I was miserable right up to the delivery. I did an assessment. Every day I thanked God for saving my life, getting me off the streets, and doing reconstructive surgery. Although I bleed, I have the best doctor in the universe. I have faith that this operation will be another one of his wonderful creations, but most of all I thank God for his revelation. I don't have to ask God today what's going on. He was thoughtful enough to tell me before he started. "Surgery"!

With every incision I think back to Jesus hanging on the cross and I know that he bore my sins and my sickness and as heavy as my cross was, he carried everybody's mess. This makes my trials seem so small. I remember the words of Paul, which states, "For I reckon that the suffering of this present time is not to be compared to the Glory which will be revealed in us."

Life is worth living today even with all of its trials because I know that a walk with the Lord is better than a walk with out him. When it's all over we shall shout hallelujah, we'll be going home to live with God. But there was still much more life to live, still more to go through before I would reach my destination. Not having a clue as to where this journey would end. I lay smack dab in the middle and I didn't know how to proceed. And so I reflected.

Reflection

I've become just a set of eyes watching my whole life and its dynamics just pass me by. If someone notices that these eyes are attached to a face, a neck, two hands, two feet, a pair of arms, a pair of legs and a pair of dentures, they just might figure out that all of these attachments are just a cover for one big broken heart, an empty shell that used to house my spirit and my mind. But the pain of a broken heart caused a shut down in my soul and a breakdown in my mind. The pain of my past has affected me so much that I've learned how to become invisible. If I can fit into the mold of normalcy in this society, then I would never have to hurt again. How could I hurt if I had no body, no spirit and no mind? Fitting into society meant that I could walk by unnoticed and undisturbed. It means that I can just float around and bear witness to the whole thing while never really feeling the impact of life's cruelty, and at the same token never experiencing the happiness that comes around to visit once in a while.

This method of hiding became a survival mechanism. At first I enjoyed hiding and now it has become something that I depend on. So if someone were to notice that there is a person attached to these eyes, they would always see the normal person. Not too tart, and not too sweet. Not too ugly and not too good looking. Never rocking the boat or causing a disturbance, because to bring attention to myself would mean that I was not invisible the way I wanted to believe that I was. If I was to die today, the only thing that one could remember is that I served them and served them well.

Eight years in recovery and I am just coming around to notice. Damn, I didn't just disappear when I entertained suicide. I came to this realization when my eyes met the set of eyes inside of the glass. I noticed that there is a body attached to these eyes. "No problem. I'll just avoid this glass," I thought. But, when I walked away this time, I couldn't forget. I couldn't forget the image that I saw in the glass. The age that had fallen upon my face since the last time I took a look. Every part of my face could tell a story. My ears are the instruments that caused me to hear that I wasn't good enough. My nose said that I was too black and my skin said that I was too light. So, I am here, it wasn't just a dream/nightmare. I was abandoned emotionally and I was abused emotionally, sexually, physically and spiritually and it hurts so badly. Within the word recovery, I found the word "cover" and to take it further I found the prefix "re." And for these eight years I learned how to re- cover up the wounds and move on. I learned how to pretend that the pain was not there. I remembered when I was a child. I remember how my mother placed very high standards on my life. She told everyone how smart I was and I was always expected to be extraordinary.

I remember being so afraid of failure. I was afraid of letting my mother and my grandparents down. I hated competition. It was there for the sole purpose of reminding you of how good you were or that you were not good enough. When I was faced with a challenge I ran, because the ideas that my mother had about her good little girl were not the same as the ones my peers had. I fell somewhere in between. The girls in school always said you think you're cute, you think that your hair is long; you think you're smart." I never realized that I was cute, I was smart and I had long hair. I had no idea of how to handle this situation.

I had no interaction in the home with a sibling and I had underdeveloped social skills. I wanted to be like other kids who were just normal kids that had friends and their parents loved them whether they were smart or not so smart. When kids wanted to fight me, I didn't know how to defend myself. I knew that if I would fight, I would get into trouble. Why not just disappear? I managed to disappear quite well. I believed that I was successful. I thought that no one could see me. Or at least they acted that way.

I had become adjusted to normalcy and then one day my mother got married. As invisible as I tried to be every once in a while I would somehow bump into my stepfather's fist. I was reminded by the tears as they made contact with my cheeks that are made to smile, but they were part of the mask that I used to cover the dentures that I hardly clean, because to me they weren't suppose to be there.

Eight years in recovery reminds me of the eighth month in pregnancy. In the fifth month even though you are pretty much developed on the outside, God is still developing the inside and you are considered premature.

So in the eighth month you are considered to be coming any day now. At this point God is preparing you for your new environment. My tears remind me of the leakage that proceeds the bursting forth of the living waters. The things that I have lived on for the past eight years will no longer sustain me in my new world. The cord represents my dependency on people, places, and things. I will no longer need these old connections in my new life. Although the cord was vital to my development thus far, I will have a new connection that will not limit me to the small space that I have become accustomed to. I know now that I am about to be delivered. The discomfort of my present environment tells me that I have outgrown my protective sac.

The stirring of everyone around me represents the contractions of the walls that contain me. Me, I am laid inside the wound and I am starting to recognize that I have hands and feet, arms and legs that I did not develop so this lets me know that I am not alone even though it appears to be that way. I am made to know that when I am delivered the only one for me is the one who is being born with me. Meaning, that no one could tell my story like I could. No one has seen what these eyes have seen the way these eyes have seen it. People, even mother, has very little to do with the development of a fetus.

Jesus said that unless you become like a little child you would not enter into the kingdom of heaven. So I thought of an infant baby. They have hands and feet, but don't know how to use them yet. They have a mouth and don't know how to eat on their own or speak. They smile because somehow they know that they will be protected, loved and their needs will be met. Without even saying a word, mom and dad know just what he or she needs. So what God is telling me is that I have to become dependant on him fully before I can experience peace in my life. I am going to be delivered soon; I can almost see light. I am coming forth and no one has the power to stop this rebirth not even me. For if I can not come forth naturally, than God will cut everything out of the way because I am purposed to come forth.

This time I don't have to worry about being abandoned by my mother and my father again, they have already left. I have a new parent. He said that he would be a mother to the motherless and a father to the fatherless, and he promises never to leave me. I don't have to worry about food or drink, my Father is able to provide food enough and to spare and his water is so quenching that I will never thirst again. All of the things in my past are forgotten; however I have a birthmark to remind me of what it cost me to get here. I don't have to worry about falling because my father will catch me. And, when I make a mess, it is my father who will change me. For this conception was immaculate, the development was magnificent and just think, you haven't seen anything yet.

When I went into labor with my third baby, my boyfriend went to sleep, until they decided to do a cesarean section. I had never been cut in my life. But the baby was born healthy. Again, God has blessed me with a healthy baby girl. Healthy in spite of myself, in spite of the fact that she was another one born outside of wedlock and in spite of the fact that I was living in sin. Here I was with so much pressure on me, not working and living with the fear that this man would eventually leave again.

When I brought baby home, I noticed that my legs were swollen terribly; I was having dizzy spells and severe headaches. A great snowstorm had hit the city and I was homeward bound as my boyfriend, the kids and I were trying to fit into a very small space. The pressure was intense.

Two weeks later, I went to the hospital to have stitches removed and they discovered that my blood pressure was 215 over 101. They told me that I was about to have a stroke. They immediately admitted me and I was there for a few days. They sent me home with medication and about a week later I had a seizure. I was sent back to the hospital and when they sent me home this time I had six bottles of medicine. I pushed them away after about a week and I told the devil that I don't receive this disease, nor this medication. I was immediately set free.

A month later I was back to work. It seemed as though my relationship had gotten better. I resumed the counseling that he and I had started together and I am currently attending marriage counseling alone. I discovered that I was co-dependant. God gave me an awesome revelation of Co-dependency. He told me that my boyfriend is an addict. He drinks. The spirit of addiction is present, stronger and stronger as long as he feeds it. Then when I sleep with him, the spirit was transferred to me (A once recovering and now delivered addict). Since God has shut the door to my past and promised me that he will never allow me to go back to a substance. I attached myself to the addict.

A Co-dependant person is addicted to the addict. With that I was able to address my issues. I was able to treat my sickness no different from my addiction to drugs. I found out how to separate myself a day at a time, and I remained in this relationship. I was able to somehow manage myself inside of it. My therapist, Arnold Sell, was able to separate me from my anger. He caused me to see that I was an individual and not just some product of everyone else's stuff. Even though my emotions had calmed down a lot, I was still left with a void. This is where I heard the voice of God telling me that he wanted to deliver me, not just recover me. I watched addicts that had ten years or more, go back to drugs and finally I could see why. Even though the aggravation of active addiction was over I still had to deal with a very messed up me. So clean I had to see that I was a mess. I had to make some of the same bad decisions in recovery to see that I was in need of a savior and not just a twelve-step program.

Chapter Seventeen

THE WEDDING

On August the 23 rd of 2003 I married the man I love. I decided that I no longer wanted to live in sin. I figured that even if this was a mistake that God would never fix it as long as I lived with this man unmarried. The wedding day was so beautiful. I stood at the door as a young man sang "To God Be The Glory." Tears filled my eyes as my ex-mother in law stood at the door with me. I thought she was going to give me away. I walked down the isle with my grandfather. I saw my husband looking at me with adoration. He was so fine in his long-tailed black suit. He was smiling with his million-dollar smile and I couldn't wait to be joined to him. It wasn't until I was walking down that isle that I realized that I was being set free. It was then that I realized that I was entering into a new covenant with the Lord Jesus. It was then that I realized that God was blessing me and that he would honor this walk of faith, and bless me because I wanted so much to please him.

I knew that my ministry wouldn't go anywhere as long as I was living in that lifestyle. I realized that I wanted more of Jesus, so when I sought the kingdom and his righteousness, not mine, God gave me the man that my heart desired to be my husband and we were joined in Holy Matrimony. I had written a poem for my wedding and my daughter read it. It went like this:

When God created Adam
The first relationship had begun
And God decided that it's not good
that man should be all one

Lay down Adam and when you rest
I'll take a mate from out of your side
Bone of your bone and flesh of your flesh
She shall be your loving bride

Adam you will cherish her and meet her every need
And into this woman you shall plant a very precious seed
And as long as you trust me, no one will impose
Out of all of my creation, for you, this is whom I chose
And now I'll give to you this woman
To love and honor and be your friend
This will be an anointed union
the three of us in sweet communion

Adam went to sleep and when he had awaken
He felt for the rib that God had taken
And before him was his lovely bride
That God had taken right from his side
He rubbed his eyes in disbelief
She brought him joy and much relief
He spoke to her and she replied
"I'll forever be by your side"
Never had I anticipated this

I am overwhelmed with bliss
While keeping our eyes on Jesus Christ
God was making us husband and wife
While walking with God and holding his hand
God was working his wonderful plan
It was more than we could ever wish
He took two people to make one flesh
I finally have everything I want
My life is so complete
I have someone to hold my hand
While sitting at our savior's feet

Someone who knows the word of God
To minister to me when times are hard
What did I do to deserve this reward?
I waited and trusted in the Lord

Someone to walk by my side
With Jesus as our marriage guide
Someone to pray and intercede
And provide for me when I'm in need
Someone to hold me day and night
And make sure everything is all right
Lord we owe it all to thee
For our love is a ministry

And though it's a mystery
How we stayed together
Through sunshine and rain
And the stormy weather
Through enlightening
And the roaring thunder

Our love is a mighty wonder
And that which God has joined together
We'll let no man put asunder

It was as though God opened a window and truly poured out his blessing that day. After we said our vows, my father and his wife came in. I was so surprised to see them, because I heard that she was ill. They thought enough about me to show up. My mother's sisters and my cousins whom I was sure had forgotten all about me, they showed up and decorated this small community room as if it were the Sistine Chapel.

My grandparents were there, my sister was at my side and most of all my stepfather was there. He told me that he loved me and that he was so proud of me. You couldn't imagine the feeling that I had from that uninvited guest. Someone that I felt had hurt me. Someone from whom I craved approval, and then later validation, telling me what I needed for a healing deeper than I ever imagined or even thought possible. And I was so grateful. I am grateful that God knew what I needed and he made it possible. If God had shut my eyes that day and took me home, I felt so whole and so complete that I would have left here so willingly.

After this I managed to find myself back on the job where I was the executive assistant, but only, as a Client Service Rep. This was a demotion. This was where I started and I asked God why? He told me "Remember when I told you promotion? I gave it to you and you went to the hospital making more money than you ever made. You were so high and so proud that when I sent the gay guy and the dope fiend for you to minister to, you were so intolerant and you moved on. Didn't I deliver thee from both of these things? I answered yes. It was clear to me then that at least a great part of the surgery was over. The bypass was almost complete. I had learned how to depend on the Father, The Son and The Holy Spirit. I had learned how to treat people with love and respect. I learned how to humble myself and give God the praise for everything in my life. I learned how to love my self and I learned how to forgive myself as Christ had done so very long ago. I discovered God's mercy and that allowed me to be merciful. I discovered God's purpose for my life and in Him I found the courage to live again. From that position that I felt was below me, I found a job through someone that I happened to talk with on the phone. I'm now making more money than ever. I live with my husband and my three girls and we are working on becoming a family. My grandparents are alive and well, thank the Lord. It's wonderful to be alive. All because of a man named Jesus, that loved me so much that he saved my life. You see the intervention was divine. A lot of what we do here is choice, but every now and then, God steps in and intervenes whether you want him to or not. When this happens no one understands, not even you. You listen as folk question, "Why you?" as you agree with them. But the Father told me that many are called, but few are chosen. I thank the Lord that he chose me. As painful as my process has been, I bless the Lord for every minute. For how he saw what I didn't and did what was best in any situation. I'm not perfect, but I know that I've been changed. I know that God will continue this work until his return. I'm free from the guilt and the shame. He said he is faithful to forgive me. I thank God for the opportunity to share my life with others. It was hard enough to have God share it with me. I am delivered and I thank God for the freedom. I'm 38 years young and for the first time I know how it feels to be free. I owe it all to him.

Epilogue

I sat on this book for a long time. I guess what I was waiting for was the perfect ending. But there is no perfect ending especially when you're at the beginning. I wanted to make my life a rags to riches story. A saved-by-my prince on the white horse type of fantasy. But that's not my reality. I was supposed to have died and gone to hell. But, I'm walking around and able to give my God Praise for saving my life. The blessing is in my children; knowing that I could have destroyed them before they were even born, but they are here, and they are healthy. My two oldest are both honor roll students. And I have another chance at raising them. The blessing is that I have a new husband that loves me, where I used to believe that I was so unlovable. The blessing is that I am employed today, I can use the experience to develop my entrepreneur potential. The blessing is that once I was hopeless, now I have hope. Once fearful and now I have courage. Once in bondage and now I'm free. Once dead, now resurrected. Once a sinner; now saved by grace. The best thing of all is having a relationship with my Savior. That is more than the entire world to me. But if it will make a more interesting ending, take this: She lived happily ever after.

Thank You Jesus!